AF881870

THE THRIFTY AUTHOR'S GUIDE TO

Selling and Promoting Your Book Online

Gail Z. Martin

Comfort PUBLISHING

The Thrifty Author's Guide to
Selling and Promoting Your Book Online

All rights reserved. The author guarantees all contents are original and do not infringe upon the legal rights of any other person or work. No part of this book may be used or reproduced, stored in a retrieval system or transmitted in any form or by any means without prior written permission of the publisher, except in the case of brief quotations embodied in critical articles and reviews.

For information, address Comfort Publishing, 296 Church St. N., Concord, NC 28025. The views expressed in this book are not necessarily those of the publisher.

Copyright ©2011 DreamSpinner Communications.

First printing

Book cover design
by Reed Karriker

ISBN: 978-1-936695-40-9
Published by Comfort Publishing, LLC
www.comfortpublishing.com

Printed in the United States of America

Dedication

This book is dedicated to every writer who dreams of sharing ideas, solutions or stories with the readers who need them. And of course, it's also dedicated to my family and friends who support and encourage my writing. Thank you.

Table of Contents

Author's Note

A word about the way this book works. If you read *The Thrifty Author's Guide: Launching Your Book Without Losing Your Mind* or other books in this series, you may find the first six chapters to be familiar. That's because they lay the groundwork for the rest of the advice in the book. If you're a new reader, these chapters are essential to get the maximum value from the book. If you're a returning reader, feel free to review these chapters so that the information is fresh in your mind—you'll need it going forward.

Introduction

In today's world, authors are expected to handle all or most of the marketing for their books. This is true for authors lucky enough to sign with one of the large New York publishers. This is even truer for authors who are self-published or represented by small presses.

Luckily, there's the Internet. Thanks to the World Wide Web, authors can reach readers around the corner and around the world on a minimal budget. Readers increasingly turn to the Internet to find recommendations and reviews, as well as to purchase new books. The expansion and refinement of print-on-demand technology, e-books and do-it-yourself audio formats have given readers unprecedented choices—and provided amazing new opportunities for authors.

Your website is the gateway through which the readers of the world find your book and create a relationship with you as an author. In today's wired world, readers want to make a connection with authors that goes beyond the covers of the book. Not too long ago, if a reader wanted to contact an author, it was necessary to write to the publisher, wait months for the publisher to forward the letter, and hope that the author received it. Replies were nearly non-existent.

The Internet made it possible for readers to interact with authors, and raised the level of expectations. Today, authors who choose to be absent from the Internet and unreachable, do so at their own peril.

This book will not only help you build a website that promotes your book, but it will also provide a guide for creating a site that is a user-friendly, engaging place for readers, reporters and reviewers to discover more about you and fully enter the world of your book. Most importantly, I'll help you avoid the most common mistakes authors make, and share secrets, tips and great ideas to make your site a powerful marketing tool. Let's get started!

Chapter 1

Online Marketing Is Now the Author's Responsibility — and Opportunity

Congratulations! You've finished writing your book, and you've either found an agent who found a publisher, or you've arranged for a publisher yourself. That means the hard part is over, right? Wrong! In fact, the hard work is just about to begin.

For people who like to write books, writing is the fun part. Authors love to tell a story or share knowledge. Even the research and editing is enjoyable, because writers understand how it fires their imaginations. When the final editing is complete and the manuscript goes to the printer, most writers heave a sigh of relief, then collapse. They assume that the publisher or the bookstore will sell their book while they go on to the next project. It doesn't work that way.

A Great 19th Century Business

Publishing is an industry where profit margins are surprisingly slim. That's because publishing hasn't changed much since the 1800's, a problem that is only gradually being addressed. It costs a lot of money to edit, format and design a book. There's even more money involved to print it, warehouse it, ship it, and take back unsold books from bookstores.While e-books eliminate most of these problems, until they catch on with a majority of readers, authors must make do with the realities of traditional publishing. All those production expenses leave very little extra cash for marketing.

Yes, it seems like books written by celebrities get the biggest ad budgets, and they do. That's because publishers, who have paid hundreds of thousands, and perhaps even millions of dollars in advance, have to make their money back. That leaves less — or no — money to promote new authors who need the marketing the most.

The Rules of Promotion have Changed

Publishing houses have traditionally paid for expenses such as shipping huge quantities of review copies to newspaper reviewers and placing big ads in major industry magazines. Unfortunately, these tactics aren't working as well in today's Internet-driven world. Fewer people read newspapers, and many major newspapers have disappeared. Magazine readership has also dropped. Among those that have survived, many have stopped reviewing books. So the traditional, expensive, publisher-driven techniques aren't as valuable as they once were.

Thousands of citizen-journalists have created their own book review websites dedicated to every taste and genre. In many cases, these informal sites have replaced the big newspaper book reviewers. Websites, book review sites, book-themed podcasts, book-focused Internet radio shows, book-related social media sites or groups and online discussion forums have sprung up to take the place of the traditional media. There are more of these new outlets than there were newspapers and magazines, providing lots of opportunity for reviews. Best of all, writers can access these new opportunities for free.

Free = Hard Work

Let me qualify free. I mean free as in not costing money, but not free as in not requiring effort. None of the techniques in this book require you to spend money or hire someone to help you; although you may find that you prefer to do so to speed things along. The truth is that, if you're willing to invest the same kind of elbow grease in marketing that it took to write your book, you can reach a global audience for the price of a high-speed Internet connection.

Sales of mega-blockbusters, like the *Harry Potter* or *Twilight* series, and big names, like Stephen King or Clive Cussler, sell hundreds of thousands or even millions of copies. But the average book printed in the U.S. sells 7,000 copies or fewer. Many authors struggle to sell even that many copies. Now you see why web promotion becomes essential for authors who want to continue publishing, and perhaps make some money.

A Quick Recap of Publishing Reality

When you sell a book to a publisher, some authors receive a promise of royalties, unless you wrote a book that is a work-for-hire project. If you received an advance, you must sell enough books for the publisher to recoup the cost of your advance before you receive royalties. The real meaning of advance is "an advance against royalties." It's like a draw on commission in a sales job. If you don't sell enough books to earn out your commission, then you won't earn royalties. If this happens, your book effectively lost money for the publisher, who will be reluctant to buy another project from you again.

If you self-publish, you have funded the entire cost of creating your book, so you have even more money at stake. You need to recoup those costs in order to break even, and before you can consider any sales to be a profit. If you don't sell the books, you'll have invested a lot of money and have nothing to show for it but boxes filled with books. You might be hesitant to put up the funds to create another book.

Your book faces a lot of competition, so marketing is essential. Even the best-designed, best-written book shares bookstore space with tens of thousands of other titles, most of which are just as attractive. As a reader browses and sees your book, you want him to think, "I've heard of that book." Recognizing the name of your book, or the name of the author, makes it more likely that a reader will pick up your book and read the back cover. Marketing is all about creating name recognition. The web can help you do that on a global scale.

Different Authors, Different Goals

Would it surprise you to know that not every author has a goal of becoming a New York Times' bestselling author? While few people would turn down the honor if it were offered to them, there are other reasons that authors write, even a few that don't involve money.

Here are some other reasons to write a book:

1) You want to further a cause or educate people about something important;

2) You want to raise money for a charity;

3) You want to enhance your professional expertise to land more clients;

4) You are a professional speaker who needs a "back of the room" product; or

5) You are so passionate about your topic or story you want to share it.

There are also other ways besides money to define success. These can include:

1) Voicing a minority opinion or making a change in the way people think;

2) Recording something important for posterity;

3) Sharing information that saves or changes a life;

4) Providing insight or how-to knowledge on a subject with a small, but passionate audience; and/or

5) Providing a regional or special-interest view on a subject that is underrepresented.

Control Is a Good Thing

When you decide to lead the web marketing effort for you book, you're taking control over the fate of your own creation. The publisher (if you have one) is risking his investment in designing, printing and distributing your book. You as the author are risking your future as a commercially viable writer. If you're a self-published author, then you also have an investment in the boxes of books stored in your garage.

Ideally, you can work together with your publisher on marketing and website. In my experience, publishers are happy to find an author who is committed to the effort that is required to help a book rise above the average. You may find that there are some things a publisher can do that would be more difficult for you to do for yourself.

Some marketing efforts that are easiest for the publisher to do include running an ad that features several of the publisher's recent titles (including yours) in the trade journals read by bookstore buyers and publishing professionals. In addition, it can include negotiating with bookstores for better in-store placement, and creating posters or display materials. It might even include having a table at a big industry trade show or event like Book Expo of America, or one of the smaller, regional book shows where you could do a signing or make an appearance.

Some publishers really don't have the budget to do more than print the book. In that case, see if you can gather valuable contacts and suggestions from them as you embark on your marketing mission. That can include introductions to other authors who may be interested in joint promotions or shared expenses, or referrals to influential bookstore owners or library buyers who can put in a good word for you. You won't know what's available to you until you ask, so don't be shy.

In this book, you'll learn how to plan for the three critical stages of your book's birth: pre-launch; launch; and post-launch. When you have a plan, you have a road map. This means you can create activities that move you closer to your goals, and you can avoid actions that waste time and money. You have control, and that's a good thing. No one in the world cares as much about your book as you do. That's why you need to control its destiny.

Gail's Tip:

There's nothing better than connecting with readers who share your passion. Marketing enables them to find you and make that connection.

✎ ASSIGNMENT 1: Your Marketing Skills Inventory

This is where we look at what your natural abilities are, and how they can help you market your book. We'll also figure out what kinds of things you'd really rather not do. This way, you'll know what tasks you may want to outsource or just avoid (at least for now).

Look over the following list of skills. Which are you comfortable with? Which make you uncomfortable? Use a yellow highlighter for the skills you possess, and a green highlighter for the skills that aren't quite you.

Skills	Marketing Uses
Writing	Preparing press releases, media kits, blogs, articles and other PR materials
Public Speaking	Greeting the public at signings; Speaking at workshops and conferences; Doing radio interviews
Research	Building media lists; Uncovering contact information for reporters, bookstores, etc.
Internet Experience	Researching or setting up a basic website or blog; Using Internet tools or applications
Social Media	Connecting online on Facebook, Twitter, MySpace and book-related sites
Organization	Setting up signings and appearances; Maintaining your contact list; Scheduling promotions
Graphic Design	Creating bookplates, stationery, business cards, bookmarks, posters, and a logo
Phone Skills	Scheduling signings; Pitching stories to reporters; Giving radio or podcast interviews
Collaboration	Setting up joint signings or panels with other authors; Connecting with other authors for shared publicity or shared sales promotions
Photography	Taking digital pictures or web video of your own events; Using a webcam

"Been There, Done That" AUTHOR TIP ✔

"Websites need to be used for what they are there for, book information. Dedicating a page to a bio or press release is the right thing to do, but don't go overboard. Pages of recipes, your musical tastes, long lists of links to your favorite online places or info on the hobby knitting you do isn't what the readers are there for. All those things can be incorporated into your bio page. Be concise, and informative about your work, and make sure all covers are linked as "buy nows" and your website will get more traffic that is looking to buy your book."

— *Stella Price, Award-winning bestselling author*

Chapter 2

The Rise of the Author-Marketer

No one in the world cares as much about your book as you do, not even your mother. Your publisher, your agent and the bookstore manager have lots of books and authors to worry about. As much as they may like you and/or your book, their time is shared with other authors and professionals. Your book's future depends on you.

Before the Internet, most readers never gave much thought to actually meeting the author of their favorite book. Outside of occasional local book signings, library readings and a handful of literary festivals, authors were a solitary lot, toiling away alone in an office. Big name authors might get interviewed on TV, but not often. Readers who wanted to contact an author had to mail a letter to the publisher, and then hope the publisher would forward it to the author.

Everything changed with the Internet. People can now connect with each other in a whole new way. Authors don't have to wait to be invited onto a talk show, nor are they limited by geography to meet only the readers within driving distance of a bookstore or library. However, the Internet has also raised expectations. Because the means exists to connect, there has become an increasing obligation to do so. Now, writers who aren't actively communicating with readers are noted for their absence. In marketing, absence is never a good thing.

It might be nice to think that your book will rocket to the top of the bestseller lists on its own strength. But the truth is, people will never read that wonderful book if they don't know it exists. And, the best resource to help them find it is you, the author.

Reaching the Two Key Audiences

Book marketing requires reaching out to two key audiences: the media and the reader.

The Internet has opened up new opportunities to accomplish this, and made it less expensive. To promote your book successfully, you need to understand how these two audiences differ, and why you'll have to approach each group a little differently. Your website can help you reach both groups.

The Media

Under "media" you can include both online and offline book reviewers, reporters for newspapers and magazines, bloggers, webmasters, librarians and bookstore owners. Media also include TV and radio hosts, podcasters, Internet radio programs, and even Twitter users with large followings. These are the gatekeepers who decide which books get mentioned and which books don't. They make recommendations to readers and customers, and they can drive sales up in large quantities.

You can think of these individuals as influencers, because their opinions influence others on whether or not to try a book. Not only that, but some of these influencers determine whether your book will be available at all. If librarians or bookstore owners don't think your book will be in demand, they won't stock it.

Selling your book isn't the media's goal. Their goal is to inform and entertain their customers or audience. A reporter who doesn't inform and entertain loses a reader. When a radio host doesn't inform and entertain, the listener changes the channel. The same is true for online media such as podcasts and websites. Audiences have very short attention spans, and very little patience with anything that doesn't interest them. So reporters, reviewers, bloggers and radio/podcast hosts are always looking for something new and different that relates directly to their audiences' needs. You as an author have to shift your thinking from, "how can I sell my book?" to "how can I hook the audience's interest with some useful information and entertain at the same time?"

The best way to do this is to link your topic to something everyone's already talking about — current headlines. If you're the author of a financial book, and the headlines are about a recession, pitch yourself as an expert on sticking to a budget, getting out of debt, or saving money in unexpected ways. If you've written a fiction book about a messy divorce, watch for a big celebrity break-up to talk about pre-nups, betrayal and private investigators.

I write a fantasy adventure fiction book series about ghosts and magic. You might think that someone who writes this genre would have trouble finding current headlines. However, just as I was getting ready for my second book tour, *Newsweek* published a poll showing that 77% of Americans believe in the supernatural. That study became the hook for my media pitches, helping me to land interviews for radio, podcasts, blogs and newspapers all over the world.

Gail's Tip:

Informing or entertaining is a must. Informing and entertaining is a home-run!

How do you find the media? This is where you have a choice between elbow grease and cash. You can buy media lists from organizations, such as ParaPublishing, that are compiled especially for book promotion. These lists can save you a lot of time, but they may not be tailored to your genre or your special niche. You can also compile a list yourself — an approach which is time consuming but thorough. You can hire someone to compile the list for you (not necessarily expensive if you find an assistant through Elance.com or Craigslist.com). Or, you can hire a PR agency to promote you to the media list it has compiled.

Obviously, the least expensive option is to compile the list yourself. Getting hands-on experience in list building is a valuable exercise. I advise doing at least some of your own list building because you'll learn a lot about what's available, and how the sites differ. The information you need is on the web. You'll also get an idea of how many of each type of media are out there. This includes the number of chain and independent bookstores near you, as well as library branches. You'll also need to adjust your pitch for the personality of each host, reporter or site and make changes depending on whether you're contacting an interviewer, a librarian or a book store manager.

The Reader

We live in a "do-it-yourself" society. We've been trained to bag our own groceries, pump our own gas, and even update our own records at the doctor's office. So it should be no surprise that consumers now get their own news. In the pre-Internet days, you had to wait for the daily paper, the monthly magazine, or the six o'clock news. Today, consumers go to the Internet to get the information they want, when they want it — 24/7.

In fact, today's consumer goes around traditional media in an increasing number of ways. If you don't want to be bothered by ads during your favorite TV show, just TiVo it and skip the commercials, or wait for the season to come out on DVD and get it from Netflix.

Can't stand radio commercials? Plug in your iPod. As for newspaper and magazine ads, an increasing number of readers get their information from online editions, bypassing the paper format entirely.

So, while the media remains an important part of spreading the word about your book, they aren't the only game in town anymore. That means that it's essential for you as an author to make it easy to find out about your book online. Here are some key ways to do that.

» **Your own website** — This should be a home for everything about you and your books.

» **Search Engine Optimization (SEO)** — Figure out the keywords that readers look for to find a book like yours. Which words would they type into Google if they don't know your name or the book title? For example, would it be budget, quick dinners, or even vampires? Use a tool like Google Keyword Tool (it's free) to see which keywords get the most hits. They are the words you want to use in your website copy, your press releases, and anything you post online. Those words will work the best for helping your information come up closer to the top of a reader's search.

» **Social media sites** — Facebook, MySpace, Twitter, Shelfari, GoodReads, AuthorNation, BookMarket.ning and many other sites create online communities where readers and authors can connect. Readers can ask questions to authors, comment on books, post their own reviews, and refer friends to books they like.

» **Online PR sites** — Some of these sites are free, and some require a fee. The benefit of posting your press releases on these online distribution sites is that it creates more links to your book website. Search engines, such as Google, like to see lots of inbound links.

» **Web audio and video** — Posting a short video to YouTube is free. A good YouTube video can reach millions of viewers who are actually interested in the content (not heading out for a sandwich, like they do during a TV commercial). With a webcam, it's easy to record yourself, upload the video to YouTube, then put a copy of the video onto your website. Programs like AudioAcrobat make it just as simple to record a greeting, or even a short reading from your book. Then you can put that link on your homepage, attach it to an email, or post it on your blog.

» **Your own blog** — A blog can be a great place to continue a conversation about your books. If you write nonfiction, you can blog on related topics and tie-ins to headline news (remember, your job is to inform and entertain!). Fiction writers can blog about everything from the process of writing to providing "how-to" information for would-be authors. Readers feel that they get to know you through your blog, and today's consumer wants a relationship, not a sales pitch.

Remember, your voice is your book's voice. You can be your book's best friend by connecting effectively with media and readers through free, online tools.

✎ ASSIGNMENT 2: Topics for Media and Readers

• Brainstorm a list of topics that are related to your book. For example, if you've written a book about fitness, topics might include: weight-loss, looking good, health, staying young, reducing the risk of disease, etc.

• Next, create a table like the one below. Take each of the topics from your brainstorming list and decide whether they are best for media or readers. (Hint: You may need a slightly different angle for media than for readers.) Then, look for something in current news headlines to make your topic relevant and hot. Here's an example table from a hypothetical fitness book:

MEDIA TOPICS	READER TOPICS	NEWS HOOK
Out of shape employees cost companies more in health expenses	Save money by getting fit	National obesity rates; Rising health insurance costs
Gyms see spike in work outs as pink slips increase	Trim down for better job prospects	Company layoffs; Unemployment statistics

• Add two new columns to your table: Outlet and Message. Under Outlet, write down the type of media best suited for your book. (A visual story is great for TV, but something that requires a little more explanation is usually better in a newspaper or blog.) In the Message column, make notes on how you might tweak the "hook" to suit the characteristics of that particular media.

"Been There, Done That" AUTHOR TIP ✔

"A website that successfully sells books needs to include a number of elements that appeal to the various people who are likely to visit the site. Potential customers are one group of people you hope will stop by, so you need sales information for them. However, unlike a pure "sales page" site, a book site must also have information for the press. Because reviews, articles, and other public relations activities are a key way to sell books, your site must have information that makes it extremely easy for the press to write or talk about you. Ideally, your site should have these six key elements:

1. A home page that explains who the audience is for the book
2. Information about the authors.
3. An online media kit.
4. Content related to your book.
5. A lead-capture mechanism
6. Links to buy."

— Susan Daffron, Logical Expressions, Inc., www.logical-expressions.com; Small Publishers Artists and Writers Network, www.spawn.org; Author of 11 books, including award-winners, Publishize *and* Funds to the Rescue

Chapter 3

The Value Connection — What Readers and the Media Want From You

WIIFM stands for "what's in it for me?" In every book marketing project, there are three categories of people asking this question: the author, the readers and the media.

The Author

Every marketing action you take, every dollar you spend, and every hour you invest should tie back into one of the goals we talked about in the Introduction. If your marketing actions don't support your goals, then either your goals are wrong, or your marketing action is off-track.

It's easy to get so caught-up in all the opportunities to market your book that you stop evaluating whether each opportunity is going to help you achieve your goals. Clear goals will help you create a budget, prioritize your time, say "no" with less guilt and "yes" with confidence.

Remember, your ultimate goal is to let the readers who are interested in your particular kind of book know that your book exists so they can buy it. You're not trying to reach every reader in the world, only the readers who read the kind of book you've written. In marketing language, the readers who read the kind of book you've written are your "target audience." To market your book effectively, you must either reach that target audience directly, or have your message relayed by people who do reach them directly (the media).

How well do you know your target audience? Here are some characteristics to consider:

» Age
» Gender
» Education level
» Income level
» Hobbies and interests
» Biggest concerns/worries
» Personality type
» Preferred location for buying books
» Library usage
» Internet habits
» Other media read or watched

The more you know about your target audience, the better you will be able to put together marketing messages that appeal to them. No book is perfect for everyone. Without a clear idea of your target, you will waste time and energy promoting to those who don't buy your type of book, or focusing on media that doesn't cover your story because their audience isn't interested.

On the other hand, when you are clear about your target audience, you can uncover unexpected and authentic ways to reach out to them. This is because you know where they go, what they do, and what their other interests include.

For example, I understand my fantasy readers because I was a fan long before I became an author. I already knew that science fiction/fantasy readers love to go to genre conventions to meet authors and celebrities from favorite TV shows and movies. I knew that fans were early and intense Internet users, and were quick to adopt podcasts and Internet radio. But what I also realized was that people who like to read fantasy adventure, like to attend Renaissance Festivals. Adding appearances at Renaissance Festivals was a successful way to broaden my reach to a highly receptive audience.

The Reader

A reader wants to be informed or entertained. If his or her main goal is entertainment, then learning something may or may not be considered a bonus. However, if the main goal is to be informed, an entertaining approach is definitely a plus.

Readers who want to be informed usually need to solve a problem. For example, they may need to fix a leaky faucet, improve their credit score, apply to college successfully, get in shape, and address a health or relationship concerns. An information reader is on a mission. He or she is likely to search by topic (Remember those keywords I talked about!), and will probably read more than one book on the subject.

No one wants to read a dry, boring book. That's why a light touch is important, even in an informative book. So, if you are marketing your book to information readers, remember that they are looking for content and readability. Create marketing messages assuring the reader that your book answers their questions and is easy to read. Give your reader tidbits of very useful knowledge in a brief, easy-to-remember and fun way. Apply the information directly to real-life situations so the reader can make a connection to his own problems. Use lots of examples and colorful abbreviations to make it easy to remember.

Entertainment readers can come in two styles: pure entertainment and sneaky learners. The pure entertainment reader looks for an escape from the real world. This person is likely to be reading fiction, specifically genre fiction. Sneaky learners enjoy learning for the sheer sake of knowing new information, as long as it's presented in an entertaining way. (Think about people who watch The History Channel or readers of National Geographic.) Sneaky learners may read history, biography or "how-to" materials because they like to learn. Or, they may read fiction to enjoy learning about exotic locations, historical events, or new technology. Science fiction readers, for example, expect good scientific information. They also enjoy learning something new, as do readers of historical romance, military fiction, and other genres.

To reach the sneaky learner, you'll need a message that promises entertainment with some tantalizing new tidbits of information. For example, readers of Dan Brown's *The DaVinci*

Code enjoyed a thrilling suspense novel, but also learned a lot about church politics, ancient heresies, doctrinal arguments, and religious controversies. Authors Michael Chrichton and Kathy Reichs incorporate cutting-edge technology and science into their thrillers, stoking the armchair expert's thirst for knowledge. At the same time, they provide pulse-pounding adventure.

The Media

You already know that the media wants to inform or entertain, and would prefer to do both. But more than that, the media wants to keep their readers or listeners so that the host, blogger, reporter or TV anchor keeps his or her job. Bored readers or listeners will always go somewhere else. Whenever too many listeners stop listening, or viewers change channels, ratings plummet and heads roll. A 24/7 media cycle means the need for news is never-ending. The truth is that the media is always looking for fresh stories, and they find those ideas from press releases.

Can you share a story that will make new readers pick up a copy or click on a story link? Is your interview interesting enough to make listeners or viewers stay tuned? Will enough people need your information or enjoy your topic to build web traffic?

For the media (both traditional and online), content is a means to drive more traffic to their newspaper, magazine, blog, podcast, radio show or TV program. It's also how bookstores and libraries keep enough traffic in their facilities to stay open.

Your job as a guest is to drive traffic, whether you're being interviewed or doing a live event. So, while you are doing an interview or publicity event, it definitely pays to publicize that you'll be interviewed or appearing somewhere! The media expects that you, as an author/expert, will bring a following of readers who want to know more about your books or topic. Once they publicize you in order to retain and build traffic for themselves, you can tailor a message that meets the needs of their audience. You can also use their format to deliver a fun, informative and memorable appearance. When you deliver an audience to them, the media is more likely to invite you back. The more you appear, the bigger your audience grows, and the more in-demand you will become with the media who want to benefit from your following.

> ✎ **ASSIGNMENT 3: Reaching Your Target Audience**
>
> • Write a profile for your ideal target reader Include as many details as you can.
>
> • Do your target readers require entertainment or sneaky learning? Where will you find them aside from bookstores? How can you tie your book into either entertainment or sneaky learning?
>
> • What informative and entertaining messages can you offer to the media, based on your book?

"Been There, Done That" AUTHOR TIP ✔

"Keep it Moving...To me one of the ways to create a great website is to keep the content moving. Sure, there will always be static areas of the website (and should be, like contact info and backlist information, etc.), but new covers, new excerpts, new character back-story snippets, new original stories, and of course - great art work - are all things that make readers want to return again and again.

"One of the things that I did on the VampireHuntress.com site was to write original content "between the books," so that readers waiting on the next installment of my series had something to tide them over and something juicy to discuss. I added a linked forum and Yahoo group too, so they'd have a place of common interest to discuss anything new I splashed on the site. All of those elements combined, along with adding a rich "universe back story" and FAQs, merchandise, and in-depth character bios helped make that site interesting to people."

— *L.A. Banks, Bestselling fiction author of the* Vampire Huntress *and* Crimson Legend *series*

Chapter 4

The Real-World Truth about Book Marketing Today

Most of us know what we think we know by observing how the world around us seems to work. And for most new authors, what we know about book marketing comes from noticing what happens at bookstores and in the media for other authors.

So, this is how we think book marketing works. Major newspapers begin running author interviews or book reviews a few months before the books becomes available. Authors are on TV and radio, talking about their book and themselves. Bookstores hang huge posters to announce new books, put up signage, and move display units filled with new books to the front of the store.

We assume that the media is notified when an author will do a book signing. In our media-induced vision, fans line up an hour in advance for a good spot in line, clutching their copy of the book. The author is ushered to a prime location, where he or she begins autographing the books. Occasionally, he or she looks up to make witty conversation until the long line of fans is finally gone.

The problem with this scenario is that it is only true for the small percentage of authors who have reached the pinnacle of success. This includes authors whose prior books have established their reputation, and those who have built a following and are expected by the publisher and bookstores to sell hundreds-of-thousands, maybe even millions of copies. It's also true if the author is already famous for something else — a TV or movie celebrity, a rock star, a recognized business leader or

CEO, or even a news-worthy victim or hero. However, for the vast majority of authors, especially new ones, reality is a little different.

Months before your book comes out, you or your assistant compile a list of media and bookstores. Then, you begin to make phone calls, either pitching yourself as a guest or trying to book a signing. If your verbal pitch is intriguing, the reporter/host or the bookstore manager will ask you to send more information, including the ISBN number. This is a polite way to find out whether you are self-published. Unfortunately, unless you can verify that you have already sold thousands of copies of your self-published book via the Internet or other means, many traditional media outlets and big chain bookstores will not schedule you. Sometimes, you can get around that if you are a local author, or if your book has a local or extremely topical angle. However, the stigma in traditional channels is still highly against self-publishing.

If you are working with a publisher who has a book distributor under contract, your next hurdle is to make sure that the stores that agree to have you come for a signing will stock the book. If there is no book, then there won't be a signing. If you've self-published, this means planning to haul the books you'll need for the event in the trunk of your car. For authors who aren't J.K. Rowling, selling twenty books is considered very successful for a two-hour signing. There are a lot of factors involved, including the weather, the number of walk-in customers the store gets, and the amount of parking availability and traffic congestion. Your signing can be also be negatively affected if there is a major event competing for attention. It also matters where your signing table is located in the store.

National media covers a tiny fraction of the more than 300,000 books that are published in the U.S. each year. Your best bet is to focus on papers where you have a personal connection — hometown, current city of residence, cities where you'll be appearing at signings, your alma mater, etc. Take heart though. The Internet is bursting with blogs, special-interest websites, podcasts and Internet radio shows that cater to genre tastes.

You still need to have a good pitch to show your potential to give a good interview, or to convince the reader that you have a good book for review. It's in your favor that there are hundreds of these sites, and they're not as heavily flooded with pitches as The New York Times, so your odds are dramatically better.

Do not, I repeat, do not regard these Internet media opportunities as second-rate. Treat them with the same respect and preparation you would give to *Good Morning America* or *The Washington Post.* "New" media is the wave of the future, and many of these sites have as many or more followers as some of the struggling "major" newspapers. Be polite, show up on time, speak in sound bites and always say 'thank you.'

Bookstores

Let's get back to reality. Most bookstores are overwhelmed and understaffed. Some will put up signage about your appearance, but others won't. Some have a newsletter or a place on their website where they promote upcoming authors, but they don't always think to add you if you don't ask. It's legitimate to ask how they can help you get the word out. After all, it brings traffic to their store. A few stores may even send out monthly press releases about events. Promotion varies widely depending on whether or not the store has a dedicated marketing person, and whether that person is excited about your book.

Be aware. Sometimes a store's manager or marketing person may have a personal bias for, or against, certain types of books (for example: non-fiction over fiction, literary books over genre novels). You probably won't know if that's the case until you get to the store. You can also ask around and find out whether authors of equivalent fame are treated equally. If you feel as if the bookstore staff have disdain for your genre or topic, cross that store off your list for future promotions. (But remember that store managers and marketers change frequently and their replacements could have a different mindset.) Live and learn. Next time, choose a venue that values your type of book.

Be sure to promote your upcoming events on your own

website, on your publisher's site, and on your blog or Facebook page. Blog about your events before and after. Use Twitter to remind people and tweet during the event from your cell phone.

Most bookstores make a good faith effort to help you succeed, but marketing may not be their strong point. Always call before you show up, just in case your books haven't arrived. It helps to have a small stash of your own that you can bring if necessary, and have the store reimburse you. Sometimes, scheduling mistakes are made, or the person who booked your event leaves and forgets to tell anyone that you are coming. Calling a few days in advance of the signing can give you time to prepare for and to deal with problems.

I'd also suggest that you offer to mail or email posters, along with a press release, and even card-sized shelf-talkers about your event to the store a few weeks in advance. (A shelf-talker is a card with a thumbnail-sized book cover and a short, attention-getting comment about your book. Independent booksellers love to put shelf-talkers beneath books to draw attention. You can make great looking shelf talkers using the backside of perforated postcard stationery from an office supply store.)

You'll also want to find out where they will put your signing table. If it's not right inside the front door, ask to be moved! It's also legitimate to ask for them to make short announcements over the PA system at the beginning and middle of your signing event so that people, who are already in the store, know you're up front.

Arrive early at the store and set up. If you've brought your own books, you'll need to carry those in, as well as whatever bookmarks or props you plan to use. You'll need to arrange your table and check in with the manager. Then, you wait for people to show up. It's important to realize that few of the people you encounter will have come because they knew you were there, even with excellent pre-event marketing. It's unlikely that you'll have a line.

Remember the front-of-store book placement and the cardboard display units? Believe it or not, those cost extra —

sometimes tens-of-thousands of dollars extra. If your publisher doesn't pay for that kind of placement, the odds are against your getting it unless there is a section for local authors or it is an independent bookstore.

Posters and in-store signage will vary by store. Some stores are good about making their own. Some will put up posters if you send materials that look suitably professional. Other stores just aren't into it. Usually, if you bring your own posters and signs to use during the event, a store will display them. Make it easy for the staff. Be willing to do the placement, and take the signs down yourself. (If the store did make nice signs, you can ask to take them with you. There may be a way to salvage part of them for re-use.)

Even if no one shows up, BE POLITE to the store staff. Remember, they decide whether or not to stock your book. It's not their fault if it rains, or they have slow foot traffic. I have heard horror stories from bookstore staff about authors with attitude problems, and it's sad. If it's a slow day, make conversation with the staff. Most book store employees like to read, and they are often asked for recommendations by shoppers. Be interesting, likeable and polite, and your odds of being recommended will rise.

Media

If you have a media interview, it will probably be by phone. Find a quiet place with a landline telephone where you won't be interrupted by a barking dog or your family. Have a bottle of water just in case your throat gets dry. Avoid tapping your fingers, clicking a pen, or other nervous habits, such as swiveling in your chair. It can be heard, and creates background noise during a radio/podcast interview.

Your mood needs to be upbeat so you can focus on providing entertaining value for the reader or listener. Answer their questions, and don't say "read my book." Be ready and waiting in position a few minutes before your scheduled time, and then stay there, even if the interviewer is late. Don't be defensive or have a chip on your shoulder. The media isn't out to get you.

You are at much more risk of being ignored than railroaded. Most reporters are decent people trying to do their jobs, so make it easier on them. Remember to post a link on your site once the interview goes live.

There you have it. That's how book signings and media interviews really work for new authors. Don't be disappointed. Once upon a time, today's superstar authors were also new and unknown. As with any business, you have to pay your dues. It gets more comfortable with practice. In addition, as your reputation and following grows, bookstores and media will become more accommodating, even if you aren't at rock-star status.

✎ ASSIGNMENT 4: Preparing for Publicity Efforts

- Use the free templates, which are included with Microsoft® Word®, to make posters for your signings. Make sure to include your cover art and an attention-getting headline.

- Create shelf-talkers for bookstores by using perforated postcard stationery. Be sure to take them with you to signings, along with peel-and-stick tacky dots so you can stick the tags to the shelf.

- Post your news on your website, Facebook page and blog.

- Think about how you will engage shoppers who come into the bookstore during your signing. Start with a smile and a friendly greeting. Don't forget to offer a bookmark and invitation to stop by and check out your featured book. Be ready with a short description that emphasizes user benefits, or that has an intriguing hook.

"Been There, Done That" AUTHOR TIP ✔

"I think one of the things that I have done that has gotten the most positive response is to post free downloadable chapters of my work on my website. The potential is huge, the cost is nil and the feedback is great. You meet so many people, especially at conventions, who might be unfamiliar with your work and, as they should be due to the huge percentage of mediocre product on the shelves, are skeptical. Giving them a taste for free, at no obligation and no risk, is something that perks up ears and opens eyes. I hand over a promo card and say, "Don't trust me, go to the website and give it a read. Decide for yourself if you like it.

"When a potential book buyer goes into a brick and mortar store, his/her purchase decision is usually based upon cover art, back cover summary, and maybe the first few pages of the book. Giving away the first five or so chapters gives them a real taste, enough to know if they are going to like it or not. This puts the power in the hands of the consumer, which is great. Amazon has gotten into this with their "Look Inside This Book" feature, which, along with the customer reviews, has sure changed the way I buy books!"

— *Chris A. Jackson, Author of* Scimitar Moon

Chapter 5

Budgeting Time, Money and Effort to Get Results with Your Website

Marketing your book doesn't require a huge budget, but there are some expenses that are unavoidable. Here is a list of some basic expenses:

» Reserving a web domain
» High-speed Internet access
» Creating a basic website
» Printing business cards and/or bookmarks with your author information
» Creating posters for your in-store events
» Gas, food and lodging for speaking engagements and book signings
» Phone calls

In addition to out-of-pocket cash, marketing your book will require a time commitment. It takes time to compile your contact lists, write your marketing materials and set up events. Either you will be doing this work (time), or you'll need to hire someone to do it for you (money).

Resources can also include other valuable elements that you may use to launch your book. This can include tapping personal favors from friends or colleagues, converting a website or online profile from its current use to a book-related use. It may also mean converting "frequent flyer" miles or credit card rewards points to reduce your travel costs. Or, it could mean utilizing discount programs, coupons or other memberships to help achieve your launch goals.

Show Me the Money

Take a realistic look at your finances. How much money can you afford to spend on marketing? Remember that marketing includes printing business cards or bookmarks, making posters, maybe even hiring an intern or an assistant to help you with research. Don't be tempted to print your own business cards or bookmarks to save money. You will not look professional, and any savings will be at the expense of credibility. These need to be done right. Realize that many people decide whether or not you're "for real" by your website. You need a good one.

Shop around for a good deal on business cards, bookmarks and posters. Many authors are happy with Vistaprint.com or GotPrint.com. Don't rule out your office supply store or local printers, but be sure to investigate deals online. Make sure you understand delivery dates and shipping prices, and read the "fine print" to avoid surprises.

Once you know your budget, make sure you have some of the basics in place. If you don't already have a website, look at the cost of getting your name and your book title as a web address from a site such as GoDaddy.com. Creating a website doesn't have to be expensive. Template-driven sites, like Citymax.com, are inexpensive and easy to use, so you can create your own site and update it whenever necessary. Don't forget to account for travel and gas expenses to attend signings/events. Make sure that you also factor in the cost of a high-speed Internet connection if you don't already have one. You may even want to investigate cellular or home phone plans that enable you to make long-distance calls for free. This way you avoid a huge phone bill when calling reporters or doing phone interviews.

Where Does the Time Go?

Now, let's consider your calendar. You can use an online calendar on your computer or cell phone, or the non-technical paper approach, but choose a book-style business calendar format. I prefer a week-at-a-glance style, because it gives me room to write in hourly commitments for each day. Immediately mark out the times when you can't travel or be available for interviews, such as birthdays, holidays, family events, vacations, work obligations, etc. Remember that you'll be talking with people in different time zones. Keep in mind that evening for the East Coast will be afternoon for California, or early morning in other parts of the world.

Mark your "Launch Date." Look at the prime weekend dates that fall immediately after your launch. You will want to keep those free for signings. Look at the weeks just prior to your launch. You'll want to give yourself as much free time as possible for last-minute preparation. Reserve this time right now.

Figure out how many hours each week you can devote to marketing your book. You may want to block out an hour a day to make phone calls to media. You may want to reserve a portion of each day for emails, or as time to be available to schedule interviews. Plan ahead now to avoid scrambling later.

Your budget and your calendar will determine your geographic reach for live appearances. Can you stay overnight for an event? Can you be gone over a weekend? You may need to factor in child care, as well as family/work responsibilities.

Resourceful Use of Your Resources

Resources come in many shapes and sizes. I listed a few types at the beginning of the chapter. Here they are again, along with some additional ideas:

» A web domain, using your name;
» Your existing blogs or social media sites that could be utilized;
» Professional memberships, especially those that include online profiles or possible opportunities to speak to groups;
» "Frequent flyer" miles or credit card reward points;
» Discount memberships — either warehouse clubs, such as Sam's Club® or Costco®, or discounts you receive as a perk for membership in the Chamber of Commerce, AAA®, AARP®, professional clubs, alumni organizations or other groups;
» Rewards programs or volume discounts with Office

Max®, Office Depot®, Staples® and other national chains;
» Discounts on products or services through your bank or credit card;
» Discount websites, such as Travelocity or other reduced-fare programs;
» Friends in the business who would be willing to give you a discount or barter services;
» Access to college interns or industrious/reliable high school students, who might trade work hours for resume and portfolio experience; and
» Contacts through your neighborhood, worship center, alma mater, as well as family and personal networks.

Most of us have access to more resources than we realize. How often have you renewed a club or organization membership and not even glanced at all the "free extras" that go with the membership? Some of the professional organizations I've belonged to have offered everything from shipping discounts to specials from office supply stores and major computer brands. Credit cards often offer discounts on everything from rental cars to cell phone service. Start reading the flyers that come with your monthly bills. Also, check out the websites of the organizations you already belong to, in order to see how you can save money and leverage your dues!

Savings can come from surprising places. My grocery store's VIP customer card offers periodic rewards. I've earned wheeled luggage (handy for book tours), a gasoline gift certificate, and other perks that have helped to offset my travel expenses. Make sure that you sign up for the discount cards for Books-A-Million®, Barnes & Noble® and other stores to offset the cost of your research materials. If you'll be traveling, make sure to sign up for discount cards offered by fast food chains, national coffee shops, and quick-marts. Sign up for memberships with your favorite discount hotel chain to earn points toward free rooms or upgrades.

People are resources, too. Your cousin's teenage son might be willing to help you set up your Facebook page in exchange for an iTunes® gift card. Contacting a local university, technical school or community college might connect you with a student videographer who could create great web video at a fraction of the cost of hiring a professional. You may be able to work out barter arrangements for everything from printing to graphic design.

Don't forget the value of introductions and referrals. Ask your friends and colleagues to recommend organizations that might need a speaker, or to introduce you to their web designer and other professionals. If you're planning to travel, tap family and friends for a free night on the couch in cities where you'll be speaking or promoting your book.

✎ ASSIGNMENT 5: Finding Readers and Resources

- Make a list of all the discount clubs and professional memberships you already have.

- Visit their websites and look for the discounts.

- Check out online sources for services (such as Elance.com) and supplies (such as Ebay.com), as well as major office supply stores' websites. You may find "online only" coupons that enable you to save more.

- Ask everyone you know for referrals to the types of products and services you will need.

- Make sure to ask stores you frequent whether they offer any kind of discount, reward, or frequent-purchaser programs.

- For things you'll need frequently, such as photocopies, you may get a deal by pre-purchasing in bulk. (For example, buy a reloadable gift card that offers you a discount per copy, if you buy 100 copies up front.)

"Been There, Done That" AUTHOR TIP ✔

"An attractive and effective author website is an essential component to creating and sustaining your online presence as an author, and to promote your book. Photos, a blog, calendar of your events, testimonials, videos, links to all your social media sites, and online press kit will serve you well. Finding innovative ways to drive people to your website and engaging your visitors will keep them coming back! In addition to your website, there are others that you would be wise to consider in advancing your online presence.

1) Create a website under your name/company name, and one with your book title as the domain.

2) Create your author profile on the Amazon.com website. You can take it one step further and list your author events, display photos of the book, and your events, and testimonials you have received for your book.

3) Create a profile on Authors Den (www.authorsden.com) to create your online presence, and promote your book and all book related events."

— *Charmaine Hammond, Author of* On Toby's Terms

Chapter 6

The Web Marketing Plan — Your Secret Weapon for Success

Believe it or not, before you create a marketing plan for your book, you need to have a business plan. Yes, you will need a business plan for your book.

Why? Because what you want out of your writing career will impact how you market yourself and your book. Remember in Chapter One how there were different reasons to write a book, and different definitions of success. In order to create an online marketing plan that achieves your definition of success, you will need to think about why you're writing your book, and what you want out of your writing career.

Scenario 1: You've always wanted to be a writer. Your stories are alive for you, whether fiction or non-fiction., Writing puts you in the "zone" where you feel most alive. You want to share your stories with others. For you, writing and the story itself are the key goal.

Scenario 2: You write as a means to an end. You have subject matter expertise that is in demand, and you have back-end products or services you want to sell. For you, a book is a way to expand your professional credentials, to land bigger and more lucrative publishing and speaking contracts, and to attract more clients to buy more profitable products from you.

Scenario 3: You write about a cause to change the world. Your book could be inspirational, a "how-to" book, or even an expose´.

You are an advocate first and a writer second. Your book is a way to reach you to change hearts and minds and hopefully, policy or individual actions.

Scenario 4: You are passionate about a subject in which you've gained expertise, and you want to share that passion with others. Or, you may wish to gain credibility among others who already share your passion. Your book might be a family history or a biography, or perhaps it's a book about Shakespeare, origami, or re-enacting Revolutionary War battles. You already know it's not a book for the masses, but you want to be known and respected among your peers, and to contribute to the body of knowledge about your topic.

We have seen four different scenarios with four different goals, and four vastly different marketing plans. All books are not created equal. As you see with the scenarios above, the goal and the intended audience will make a big difference in the type of media you target, the pitch you create, and the coverage you can expect. Your goal and audience also impact your distribution decisions, ultimate income, and business objectives. They will also determine what kind of website you build. In addition, they affect the kind of book promotion that is likely to be effective.

Basics of a Book Business Plan

A "book business plan" isn't the same as you'd use to get a loan for a company. It's a shorter version that is especially helpful to use as a springboard for an on-target marketing plan. Think about which of the above scenarios comes closest to your reason for writing your book. Next, on a blank sheet of paper, do your best to answer these questions.

» What is the transformative value of your book? How does it solve a problem for the reader, or provide value (entertainment, enlightenment, ideas, etc.)?

» Describe your primary target audience in detail (age, gender, education, location, income, key concerns, hobbies, aspirations, etc.).

» Justify why this is your primary audience.
» Now, identify your secondary audience and justify its position.
» Next, identify your tertiary audience and justify its position.
» Do a SWOT Analysis. Your SWOT analysis should make clear your Strengths, Weaknesses, Opportunities and Threats. Your business plan should have a goal or action that addresses each SWOT aspect.
» What are your book's STRENGTHS and features that differentiate it from other books on the same topic?
» What are the WEAKNESSES of you or your book? (Examples could range from lacking a distributor for your book, to having less career success in your topic than competing authors.)
» What OPPORTUNITIES currently exist in the marketplace for books such as yours? (For example, during an economic downturn, books on budgeting and saving money soar in popularity.)
» What are the biggest THREATS you see to the book's success? (This could range from you suddenly getting too busy with family, health or work issues; to suitably promote the book; to having a crisis occur that makes your topic out of favor.)
» Do a "competitive analysis." What research or data gathering have you done to understand who your competition is? What threat do they pose? How do their services/audience/service areas overlap with yours, and how might you turn weak competitors into strong collaborative partners?
» Determine your annual marketing budget in dollars. How did you arrive at that figure?
» Determine your annual marketing budget in time. How did you arrive at that figure?

Once you have thought through these items, your book business plan should become more clear. If you are writing in order to promote other products or services, or to promote yourself as a speaker and/or consultant, then your goals will focus on reaching an audience of good prospects for your other products. If you are writing for the love of the story, you have a goal of selling enough books to make it commercially attractive for you to write more books (either to a publisher, or to yourself, if you are self-published). If it's the love of the topic that draws you, then you'll need a clear understanding of where there are gaps in available materials on that subject so that you can make an authoritative statement. And, if you want to change the world, you'll need to get a sense of how fresh and well-substantiated your approach is, so you can make a splash and fend off detractors.

The Book Marketing Plan

Once you have a clearer picture of your book business plan, come up with your top three business goals and put them in priority order. For example, a writer who wants to establish a sales platform may have these goals: 1) Attract media attention as an expert; 2) Establish topic/industry credibility; and 3) Fill rooms with qualified prospects who can buy products/services or back-of-the-room books. In contrast, a writer who wants to change the world might have these goals: 1) Attract media attention to a specific need/cause; 2) Create a way to organize or raise funds; and 3) Mobilize readers to take action. Your website will play a key role with all of these goals.

A writer with a subject passion might choose these goals: 1) Attract attention within the narrow niche of media focused on that particular subject; 2) Get invitations to speak at seminars, conferences and other programs pertaining to that subject; 3) Win an award, have an article or excerpt in a prestigious industry publication, or achieve some other kind of in-group recognition as a "subject master." And, a writer with a story could have these goals: 1) Attract media attention for signings or for the launch of the book; 2) Connect with readers who share a passion for that kind of story to sell books, as well as establish relationships; and 3) Remain connected to readers as the springboard to sell other books in the series. A good website can help you achieve your goals.

Once you have your business plan goals, link each goal to a specific target audiences. Some examples of target audiences include: readers, hobbyists, and professionals within an industry or specialty; academics; the professional media; new media (blogs, podcasts, etc); bookstore buyers; librarians; and conference event planners, etc.

Once you have determined a target audience for each business plan goal, it's time to match your online marketing goals to the business goal/target audience. Make it easy on yourself. You shouldn't have more than five business goals (I would suggest starting with three), and don't try to create more than two marketing goals for each business goal. Avoid the temptation to think that every goal affects every audience. As you'll see when you try to match marketing to goals, the simpler it is, the better it will be. Here's an example table for the sales platform writer:

BUSINESS GOAL	TARGET AUDIENCE	MARKETING GOAL
Attract attention as an expert	Traditional and new media	Name recognition linked to a subject
Establish credibility	Media, prospects	Become the go-to person for subject answers
Fill rooms with prospects	Event planners, prospects	Bookings to speak and attract an audience

Once you have your top-level marketing goals, now think about the specific actions you will need to achieve them. For example, considering the first goal of using the media to build name recognition as a subject expert, some specific actions might include:

» Build a list targeting all media that covers your subject;
» Write a pitch letter to obtain interviews or request reviews;
» Create a website that conveys a professional image;
» Create a presence on social media sites like Facebook and Twitter
» Develop press releases to announce achievements and events; and
» Create basic marketing materials (business cards, bookmarks, posters, etc.).

The great thing about this method is that each marketing action is tied to marketing and business goals, as well as a specific target audience. This makes it easier for you to say 'no' to opportunities that aren't really right for you (and a way to know that they aren't right). It also gives you a guilt-free reason to say 'yes' to the opportunities that are a good fit. Now that you've created your marketing plan, let's match your to-do list with the actions it will take to make your marketing happen!

✎ ASSIGNMENT 6: Starting Your Book's Marketing Plan

• Use the tools in this chapter to create a preliminary online and offline marketing plan for your book. Have a couple of trusted friends read it over and give you feedback, then revise.

• Make sure your marketing plan aligns with your business plan, and include a budget to keep you on track.

"Been There, Done That" AUTHOR TIP ✔

"Every author needs a website, preferably bearing your own domain name. If you plan to write more than one book, it's wise to set up a site with your company name (or your full name) so that you can add other books as they are published.'

"A basic site should contain the book cover and blurb, ordering information, your bio on an "About the Author" page, information about how to contact you, the Table of Contents, excerpts from reviews you've received, and a page of links. Exchanging links with other authors, organizations you belong to, resources, etc. will improve your ratings in search engines, and make it easier for potential readers to find you.

"If your book is fiction, you might want to include a short excerpt (perhaps the first few paragraphs), a page providing background on the book's setting, historical period, or even describing the main characters. For non-fiction, you may want to include information on your topic, a list of references you used (which will add credibility), etc.

"Some websites are multi-purpose. Mine promotes my mentoring services with many pages on publishing information, writing, and publicity techniques, as well as my three books and my cat's blog. But be careful to make each page distinct, and give it a title and keyword meta-tags."

— *Barbara Florio Graham, Author and publishing consultant,*
www.SimonTeakettle.com

Chapter 7

Why Do Authors Need Websites?

Your book is finally in bookstores. Isn't that enough? No, sadly, it isn't enough. Although it's a big plus if your publishing company has arrangements with a distributor to provide your books through stores, there's more to the publishing game than distribution. Readers and the media will still want to find out more about you and your books than what they'll see on the flyleaf of your book. If you're a speaker, event coordinators will want to look at your website before they issue an invitation. And if you are published through a small press or self-published, your website will become your sales lifeline.

On the Web, Your Door is Always Open

A website is your global storefront that is open 24/7. Your website never sleeps, making it the perfect way to introduce your books and yourself to readers and reporters. It doesn't matter where they are located, or what their time zone is.

Maybe your book appeals to a very large potential audience. It still has to compete with hundreds of thousands of other books for the customers' attention and wallet. A great website lets the reader "meet" you as an author and sample a few free excerpts from your books. It will also help them delve into additional information that isn't in the book itself.

At its best, an author's website is almost as good as meeting the author face-to-face, because it facilitates a relationship with the reader. People buy from the people with whom they have relationships, so it pays for authors to reach out to readers through their websites.

Perhaps your book appeals to a niche audience. Maybe your topic is very academic. Perhaps it is regionally-themed or highly technical. The Web makes it easy for readers who are interested in your topic to find you, no matter where they're located.

It's OK if there isn't a potential readership of millions for your book. You want to reach the largest percentage possible of the readers who are interested in your topic and capture them as customers. So if you've written a book that is limited in its appeal to aficionados of particular sport, hobby, historic event or other narrow topic, don't worry about creating a *New York Times* bestseller. Focus your efforts on creating a website that will draw the people who are interested in your subject right to your online door.

What Have You Done for Me Lately?

Readers are a somewhat fickle crowd. They may love your first book. However, their attention is likely to wander in the year or so that it takes to bring out a sequel. This means that you can't take it for granted that even the most loyal fans of your first book will automatically remember to buy your next book without some help from you and your website.

A great author website helps to keep your readers engaged with you between books. It also makes it easy to remind them that a new book is coming out, and to get them excited before the book ever hits stores. You can promote your book for pre-orders before it ever reaches stores. Both publishers and booksellers really like to see strong pre-order sales, because it's an indication that the book will do even better once it is on the shelves.

In today's wired world, readers want to do more than just read your book; they want to have a relationship with you, however distant. The Internet and social media make it very easy for widely separated people to have an ongoing dialogue. Since it is so easy to do, it has even become expected. Today, an author is a recluse at his own peril.

You don't have to share details of your private life, but readers want a glimpse of the person behind the story. They want to know more about your sources of inspiration, your methods of writing and research, and your thoughts on related topics. More importantly, they want you to know who they are and that they love your books. They want a way to feel that they have met you and that you have acknowledged them.

It would be wonderful if this kind of interpersonal connection could happen at book signings and speaking events. However, that's not possible for several reasons. First, you can't possibly be at every store across the world to meet all your readers. No book tour has that kind of budget. Plus, even if you had unlimited financial backing, you'd never have time to write another book.

Secondly, the number of bookstores is shrinking in favor of online booksellers. It's sad but true. The number of independent bookstores shrunk dramatically over a decade ago when the "big box" chain stores came on the scene.

Changing consumer trends are now forcing the national chains to reduce the number of stores. Consumers are turning to online sources for their books, a trend that is likely to accelerate as e-readers become even more popular. You need to be where your customers are already congregating — online.

What Is There to Say?

It's interesting that the same writers who can create books that are hundreds of pages long, stare at a website with a complete lack of ideas on what to say. The good news is that your website has no editor enforcing a page count. It doesn't have the constraints of traditional publishing, where the number of pages is partially dictated by the printing technology. There's enough room for anything you want to say, but couldn't include in the actual book. Does that start to give you ideas?

Draw readers to your site by offering bonus material. This could be a chapter or two that didn't make it into the final book because of space constraints. It could be an original short story elaborating on something that happens "off camera" in the book but which readers would find interesting. Some other ideas could include a "question and answer" segment on writing technique; or an essay on something that you touched on in your book but didn't have room to go into in depth. Readers who liked the book will love getting extras on your site — and they'll tell their friends.

Keep readers coming back for more by sharing a little bit of yourself through web audio and web video. Digital video cameras are inexpensive and make it easy to record a "welcome" greeting and upload it via YouTube. Use an online program like AudioAcrobat.com to record yourself reading an excerpt from your book, or welcoming readers to your site.

Websites are also great places to announce news (like an upcoming new book), promote your real-world book signings and speaking events. You could even hold special online events for the readers who can't see you in person, such as "live" blogging sessions.

You can entice new readers to give your book a try by offering a free download of your first few chapters. Authors who offer "free samples" find that it increases the likelihood of readers to purchase the whole book by overcoming the fear of buying something they haven't had a chance to examine.

Depending on what type of book you write, your website may be a great place to sell related products or services. If you've written a non-fiction book related to your business or area of expertise, you may offer a package of consulting services. Maybe you've repackaged tips from your book into a calendar or coaching cards, or on anything from t-shirts to coffee mugs — even custom jewelry. Your website is the place to let readers find everything related to your book for "one-stop shopping."

Build Your Author Credibility

A good website presents you as a professional. It validates your legitimacy as an author, expert and business owner (yes, writing books is a business and needs to be treated as such).

Your site should include your bio, whether you write fiction or non-fiction.

If you are writing non-fiction, make sure your bio includes your education, professional experience, awards, certifications and other resume details that reassure readers you know what you're talking about. Fiction authors still need a good bio to wow reporters and impress the event coordinators who control bookings for speaking engagements. You can cite awards that you and your books have won, mention recent speaking engagements and media appearances, note if your book has been a "top seller" in a particular category, and share reader and reviewer praise.

A good "About the Author" section helps the media and book reviewers get the details right. At a minimum, your "About Me" section should have a professional, current photo, and a short bio of your credentials. You can spiff it up with an audio or video greeting if you like, to make it more personal. Doing so helps you step off of the page and become more "real" to your website visitors.

Your website also provides a place for you to shape the conversation about your book by providing a link to your blog, an online question and answer section, or even a frequently asked questions page. If you are writing on a topic that is the least bit controversial, it's essential that you actively participate in the conversation about your book. This helps keep it from being dominated by other people, some of whom may not agree with your book, or who may want to distort your position. Your silence only enables and empowers nay-sayers, and when you don't enter the conversation, you allow others to dictate what the market is saying.

We'll talk about more content ideas as this book progresses, but this should begin to give you some ideas for how your site can bring your book to life for visitors — and give them the feeling that they've met you, too.

Why the Publisher's Page Isn't Enough

Many publishers offer a free author's page on their own site. That's a nice perk, and you should definitely use what they have to offer, but it's no substitute for your own website for a number of reasons.

An individual author's page on a publisher's website is usually limited in space and has a rigid, one-size-fits-all format. Think of it as creating a flyer that has your photo, the book cover and some basic information. Most of these pages aren't designed to let you sell from the site, or to add downloads or other extras.

Author's pages on publisher sites are also difficult or nearly impossible for you as the author to update frequently. You're dependent on the web staff at the publishing house, and they have a lot of other, more pressing, priorities. The publisher may not even manage their website internally, meaning that you would have to work through a vendor to make any changes.

There's also the question of payment. Someone has to pay for the time it takes to make the changes. The publisher will be hesitant to permit all of their authors to make unlimited changes, because the publisher will be stuck with the bill.

It's also easy to get lost in the crowd on the publisher's page, especially if you are a new author. Sure, people will go looking for the big name writers, but your page could be easily overlooked if you aren't yet well established.

Another drawback is that author pages don't have a unique domain address. A domain address is the part after the "www" in a web address. Ideally, you would use a web URL such as www.yourbookname.com and www.yourauthorname.com. You would fill-in the actual name of your book and the name under which you write for the "your name" section. That makes it easy for readers, reporters and reviewers to find you.

An author page on the publisher's site won't have a unique domain name just for you. Your address is likely to begin with the domain of the publishing house. Then it will include lots of extra letters, numbers and characters, making it long and difficult to remember.

If your only website is an author page on the publisher's site, you are also at the mercy of the publisher for your continued web presence. If they lose their webmaster or cut their budget, it could be impossible to make changes, update the page with new books, or even remain on the Web. You're limited by their template and what they can offer to all of their authors. In addition, you don't control the frequency of updates or what the page looks like.

Remember — no one loves your book as much as you do. Not even your publisher. So if you're offered an author's page on your publisher's site, by all means take it, but don't expect that it will be a replacement for a site of your own.

✎ ASSIGNMENT 7: Taking the First Steps

• Whether you are published by a small press or large publisher, find out whether you can have a free author page, and what it will take to set it up. It's not a substitute for your own page, but don't turn it down if it's available.

• Start thinking about what you want your website to look like. Visit the sites of other authors, especially those who write the same kind of books you write. Then visit sites of successful authors in totally different genres to get some fresh ideas and see what's possible. Make notes so you can remember what you like and what you don't like.

"Been There, Done That" AUTHOR TIP ✔

"Having a book website is an essential marketing component because it makes it easy to find information about your book on the Internet. Relying on the brief descriptions you provide to Amazon or other retailers limits exposure of your book. The domain is the first most critical aspect and it should be the name of the book for the "Google" factor to be effective in finding your website. I actually would change the name of my book if the domain was already taken.'

"When I determine a name for a book and then find that the domain is available, then I know I have something unique and it will not get confused with other books or information. Another reason a book website is important is because it allows news media to access more information about your book.'

"During a TV or radio interview, it is a place that listeners or viewers can be directed to get information about the book or to sign up for a special offer. In addition, when excerpts are published from your book, the online versions will include a link to the book's website and the print versions will either include your full title or the actual website for readers to search and access."

— *Sherré L. DeMao, Author,* 50 Marketing Secrets of Growth Companies in Down Economic Times, *www.50marketingsecrets.com*

Chapter 8

Building Your Website: Create a Solid Footing

Before you create a website for your book, you have some decisions to make about what the page will be named, where people can find it, how you'll build it, what it will look like, and whether it will be a do-it-yourself project or not. Those decisions aren't difficult, but it helps to know what your choices are before jumping in, since you'll want to keep your website for a long time.

Choosing an Address

If you've been on the Internet much, you've seen all kinds of names for websites. Some are easy to remember and very descriptive. For example, Tom's Restaurant might have a website named www.TomsRestaurant.com. Easy, right? But what if it had a web address such as www.Webhost.com/locations/restaurants/Toms1485972049%&? How easily would you remember that web address to check for daily specials? You wouldn't. And neither would any of the rest of Tom's customers. At most, people might find the link if they did a Google search, but it would make it hard to promote the site on business cards, flyers or key chains.

Choosing the name for your website (called a "domain name") is the first decision you will need to make. Ideally, a great website should be the name of your book (such as www.booktitle.com) or should have your own name (such as www.JaneAuthor.com). You can find out right away if a domain name is already taken by checking on GoDaddy.com, a web hosting company, and typing in the domain name on their domain name finder.

If the domain isn't already taken, then congratulations! You can buy it. But what if it is taken? There's not much you can do about it except to find a good substitute. You could use the name of your series instead of the individual book title. You could use a middle initial with your name instead of just first and last name. Try to stick with choices that would be obvious to a reader. Avoid character names, made-up words, or other "cute" choices that readers might not readily connect with you.

If it's early in the publishing process, strongly consider renaming the book, especially if the competing domain name company is a competitor or offers similar products or advice. Not only do you not want to confuse readers who look for you and find someone else, but you also want to avoid the possibility of being sued for copyright or trademark infringement.

If your first choice domain name is taken, visit the site to see what kind of business is represented. One way to differentiate yourself is by adding a descriptive word at the end of your domain name. So if you wrote a book on do-it-yourself home repair called Handy Tips and the domain www.HandyTips.com is taken by a company that sells frozen sirloin tips; then you could adjust the site name (and possibly change the book title) to be www.HandymanTips.com, HandyFixItTips.com, or even HandyTipsBook.com. When possible, make it as different as you can from existing sites.

You can change a book title, but it's harder to change your name. Some options are to go with your full first name (Maxwell instead of Max, for example) or to shorten a full name to a common nickname (Max instead of Maxwell). Add a middle initial, or use both first and middle initials. Or, use your full first, middle and last name. You could also use your first name, last name and either the word "books" or "author" if the other person with your name isn't also in the book business.

You'll see a lot of different suffixes to the domain name: .biz, .net, .tv, as well as .com. Some people recommend taking all of them so that someone else can't grab up the variations. That's great if you have lots of extra money, but remember that you pay for domain names annually. So, if you have to just pick one domain then pick the .com version.

Equally important, since most people look for .com by default, if the only domain with your first choice of wording is already taken for .com, don't grab the .net or .biz version. It will make it much harder for people to find the right site. Choose another domain name.

Take a moment and think about future books and future product spin-offs. For example, a website with the name of your book series might be more versatile than a site with the name of just one book. Likewise, if you offer related products or services, think about purchasing spin-off site names like www.YourNameCoaching.com or www.YourNameProducts.com so that people can find your other products easily. You don't have to create sites for those names right away, but once you buy the domain and pay the annual fee, no one else can take it.

A word here about "free" sites that come with your email address, or through Google or other online services. These sites are "free" because they require you to have a banner ad at the top, and you'll have no control over who advertises there. So your book on diet tips might have a banner ad for a fast food restaurant at the top, or your book on saving money could have a casino ad.

With free sites, you get what you pay for. Not only do you not control the ad, but the domain address is usually full of gobbledygook letters, numbers and characters, making it impossible to remember. Domain names are cheap. Buy one.

Find the Host with the Most

Websites need to "live" somewhere. In reality, they "live" on a big computer server with high-speed connections to the Internet, tended by knowledgeable people who know how to keep the servers up and running so that your website stays visible to the world. Unless you own a very large company and an industrial-sized network of computer servers with a full information technology staff, hosting is not a do-it-yourself project. You will need to find a host so that your domain name and your web page have a computer address.

Fortunately, many companies offer hosting packages. GoDaddy.com is one of many hosting companies, as are Aplus.net, Vendhost.com and others. Check out several hosting companies and compare features and prices, making sure that you understand the services being offered. (If you are working with a web designer and this part is completely foreign to you, then ask for help.)

What really matters is the annual hosting fee and how much storage space you get for that fee, as well as any extras such as free templates, free email addresses and free set-up. Getting email addresses linked to your site is important, because it's much more professional to use an email address like Jane@JaneAuthor.com than to have a free email provider like AOL, GoogleMail, Yahoo or HotMail. If you go with a basic hosting package, make sure you can easily upgrade if you need more storage or advanced features.

Designer or Do-It-Yourself?

When you create your author web page, you will have to decide whether you want someone to help you design the page or whether you will do it yourself. Realize that regardless of who does the work, the page must look professional or you will damage your reputation. Having a local teenager build your site is usually a bad idea because while it might function, it will probably lack the look and feel of a truly professional site. Your alternatives are to hire a web designer or to pay the hosting company to set you up with one of their standard templates, if you don't want to do it yourself.

If you have your heart set on a site with lots of custom graphics, then you'll probably need to hire a web designer. You can find web designers through a Google search or on places like Elance.com, where you can hire a freelancer or a company from anywhere in the world. Prices, experience and aesthetic ability vary tremendously, so know your budget up front and avoid adding extras that can increase the cost.

If you just want a nice, basic site that has your photo and the book photo and your logo colors, the hosting company may be able to create a serviceable site for you using its slightly-customized templates. You won't have a site that looks exactly like anyone else's, but you may notice a pretty strong family resemblance to other sites created by the same host. This can be a good, affordable way to get started. You can always upgrade later.

If you're pretty comfortable with regular computer programs like Microsoft PowerPoint® and Microsoft Word®, don't rule out do-it-yourself template programs without checking out the options. Sites like Citymax.com make it very easy to use their templates to build a site in a few hours. You can customize the site's colors, add photos and logos, and choose from a variety of layout styles just by pointing and clicking. These sites should also make it pretty easy to put your finished site on the Internet without you needing to know the technical details of how it happens.

There are pros and cons to either approach. Whether you do it yourself or work with a designer, you'll still have to do certain crucial parts of the job. This includes:

» Determining the overall look you want — preferably a look that ties in well with your book cover. Use matching colors and design elements to pull the book and website together. Make sure your type fonts are compatible.

» Writing the web copy and making sure to use popular key-words whenever possible to increase search engine visibility.

» Supplying the dates/locations of upcoming events, recent press releases, a current photo and an up-to-date bio.

» Thinking through what content should be on the site (excerpts, a free bonus download, extra material, video, audio, etc.) so that the site is attractive, flows logically and loads quickly.

» Scouting what other authors are doing to get ideas and adapt those pieces to suit your own book and personality.

» Finding a mix of copy, photos, audio and video that enables visitors to your site to fell that they have met you and begun a relationship.

Here are the benefits of working with a designer:

» A good designer understands how people navigate websites and can advise you so that your site is user-friendly and looks up-to-date

» A good designer will also optimize your site so that pages load quickly and can be found easily by search engines.

» When you use a designer, you don't have to worry about the details of layout and artwork.

Of course, there are also potential problems to working with a designer:

» If you're not clear with instructions or take an "I'll know it when I see it" approach, be prepared for lots of extra expense and multiple rounds of revisions.

» You'll need to pay for the designer's time every time you want to update the site.

» If the designer goes out of business, you will need to have copies of all the passwords so someone else can take over.

» Designers usually work with multiple clients, so your job may have to wait its turn.

Using a template program to do-it-yourself has these benefits:

» You can change the design as much as you want to get it right without paying extra.

» You can update the site any time for free.

» Templates usually have a modern feel and a variety of graphics, so the site should turn out pretty well.

» You have total control over when your changes happen and how quickly new information is added.

» Many template programs have basic shopping cart pages so you can sell your own books and products.

But there's also a downside to doing it yourself:

» If you aren't fairly comfortable with computers, you may not understand the set-up choices (this isn't a deal breaker, since most template sites have customer service).

» You may not have time to create a professional looking site and make changes.

» You may accidentally create a site that takes a long time to load or is difficult to navigate.

» You may not know how to add the hidden tags that help search engines find your site.

» You may never quite get the site to look the way you want it to look.

The choice between using a designer and doing it yourself shouldn't scare you. Many people create their first site with a simple template program and then move up to getting help as the budget permits. The important thing is to get a reasonably professional site onto the Internet and keep it fresh with new material.

To Blog or Not to Blog

A blog (short for "web log") is a different kind of website than the traditional home page. Blogs are designed to be easy for anyone to update, and have a pretty straight-forward template with the blog in the middle of the page and sidebars of other information at the edge. They don't offer quite as many design choices, but that can create a very simple, clean look.

The heart of a blog is the center section, where the site owner enters content (just like using a word processing program). Many blogs, such as WordPress.com, are free to set up. (Check the rules — not all programs permit business-related blogging, and promoting your book is a business.) Most blogs also make it pretty simple to include a photo or a link to a video and it's easy to add pages for an "About Me" section.

Blogs have become very popular because they're so easy to update without any special computer knowledge. It's also possible to use your blog to update content to a website or to social media sites like Facebook or LinkedIn by using an application called RSS (Really Simple Syndication).

RSS is a free tool that makes it easy to link your other pages to your blog so that when you post on your blog, it updates the other sites without additional work from you. Not only do all your sites benefit from fresh content, but you get to write once and have the content used in multiple places.

Unfortunately, blogs aren't a good main website for authors who sell their own books or who want to sell related products, because stand-alone blogs (at least right now) don't have a shopping cart page.

If you want your website to be easy to update yourself but still want the extras of a designer or template page, consider incorporating your blog into a regular website. A designer will know how to do this, and many templates allow you to use RSS to feed your blog to your site. A hybrid page like this allows you to have the best of both worlds: a flexible site that can incorporate a shopping cart and other design elements while being easy for you to add content whenever you have something to say.

✎ ASSIGNMENT 8: Getting Your Website Started

• Using a site like GoDaddy.com, explore choices for your domain name and write down the best options. Take a look at the hosting plans, and make sure you understand the fees involved.

• Check out the options for building your own site using a template program like Citymax.com and compare costs and options to the price of having a custom-designed site or using the hosting company's services to build your site.

"Been There, Done That" AUTHOR TIP ✔

"If a marketing writer uses the word, "sizzle," as in "we'll make your text sizzle," I suggest you flee like a cow being chased by a McDonald's truck. Why do almost all Internet marketers insist on using the word, "sizzle," as if this was a word that they alone invented and that no one else ever used? For some reason, I see this "sizzle" word all over the place as if it is supposed to make one's text stand out from the rest.'

"All I can say to that is: "Moooooo!" The only thing that should be "sizzling" is a fajita platter, a crackling rice soup, or a giant singing cockroach in India. The moral of this story is to stay away from marketing writers who use recycled teasers …unless you actually like giant singing cockroaches.

"The other moral is to make sure your copy is intriguing, engaging, and entertaining. What funny or clever hook can you begin with to hold a reader's attention? And make sure to include keywords in your mix. (You can find them for free by doing a Google search on the term, "keywords"). When you're writing marketing copy, don't just think outside the box–flatten it!"

— *Randy Peyser, CEO, www.AuthorOneStop.com*

Chapter 9

Building Your Website: Leading Readers Down Your Yellow Brick Road

On the web, content is king. Visitors to your website expect the site to look professional, to have graphics that load quickly and that make sense with your type of business, but it's what you actually say and offer on your site that leads to sales.

In The Wizard of Oz, Dorothy followed the "Yellow Brick Road" to find a wizard who would solve her problems. Your website should provide visitors with a compelling pathway to the content that helps them find what they most desire. For non-fiction books, that means helping them understand how your book solves a problem or opens up possibilities for them. For fiction books, it's the allure of a wonderful escape into a world with action, adventure, romance, humor and memorable characters.

As you know from the previous chapters, your website is important to help you attract new readers, as well as stay in contact with existing readers. It should also be used to impress reporters and reviewers who stop by to check you and your book out to assure that you're legitimate. For many authors, a website is also where you will also sell your book and offer related products, such as coaching programs, t-shirts or mugs, etc. Your website needs to be working for you 24/7 to help you make sales and get great publicity.

That's why content is so important. At a minimum, your website should provide visitors with these essentials:

» A compelling reason why buying the book will solve a problem or provide a benefit

» Enough about you for them to recognize you as a professional and expert
» A free sample so visitors can do the online equivalent of browsing through the book in a bookstore.

Other ideas for content that will help keep your site fresh and keep you in contact with readers include:
» A bio with relevant details
» Web audio/video
» Automatic updates from your blog or podcast
» Link to Facebook, Meetup and Twitter sites
» Q&A, author interviews, bonus goodies
» Free download to build your opt-in (permission-based) email list
» Upcoming events
» Photos and comments on past events
» Extra content
» Forum for discussions or comments
» Link to Amazon
» Sales page

Unfortunately, instead of being the "Yellow Brick Road," too many websites are dead-ends filled with broken links, outdated information, incomplete or hard to follow content, confusing navigation and slow performance. When would-be readers encounter any of these hurdles, they leave the site, usually without buying anything.

Creating the Road Map

The trick is to woo prospective readers and make your current fans come back for more. To do that, it's important to have a plan before you put up your site. Here are some things to consider:
» What path do you want readers (and potential book buyers) to take through your site?
» Which pages do you want reporters or reviewers to find immediately?

» How will you persuade browsers to become buyers?
» What will you offer existing readers to build your relationship with them?

Remember that visitors to your website want to find information quickly. That means that there should be a logical route to the important pages for 1) new readers, 2) reporters, 3) reviewers and 4) current readers. Spend some time answering these questions for each type of visitor:

» What information would be most important to this visitor?
» What questions do they have that I can answer?
» How can I engage them to encourage them to buy, stay in touch, interview me or review the book?
» How can I reward them for visiting me?

Once you have answers to these questions, think about how to organize this information. Ideally, you should have a different destination page for each type of visitor so you aren't asking one type of reader to wade through information unrelated to their interests. Here are some tips to make your "road map" easy for visitors to follow:

» Name a page for each type of visitor, for example, "new readers," "current readers," "media," "reviewers." Use these page names in your site navigation so visitors can go immediately to the pages that are meant for them.
» Make the paths through your site short and clear. Try to make it possible to reach the visitor's desired destination in three clicks or less.
» Limit the number of links that go back and forth between your pages. Lots of internal links make pages difficult to update and can lead to broken links and error messages.
» Plan to have some pages be easy for you to update (like a blog) so that you can change information that quickly becomes dated, such as upcoming events.
» If visitors will be encouraged to purchase books or other items from your website, make the shopping cart easy to find

and test it yourself to make sure it is easy to use. Any shopping cart page that requests credit card information must have a secure "https" address (look for the padlock symbol.)

It's easy to get so caught up in adding pages that you lose sight of how lengthy and complicated a site becomes. When you have a draft of your site ready, have a couple of friends help you check to see how user friendly it is by giving them a list of items or specific information to find and then watch them as they search. Do they become frustrated? Can they find the information quickly? Did they run into links that were broken or dead-end pages that kept them from getting back to previous pages? Did the shopping cart work and was it easy to use?

For your website to be successful, it needs to be easy to use and friendly. Its layout should be professional looking so that they can find what they want and feel comfortable trusting you with their payment.

✎ ASSIGNMENT 9: A Great Website Requires Research & Planning

• Visit sites of other authors who are established and successful to get an idea of what you like and what you don't like from their sites. Try to pick authors who write the same general type of book as yours (fiction, self-help, specific kind of non-fiction, etc.). Make a list of the things you want to use on your site and what you want to avoid.

• Plan your road map by grouping related content together on pages that easily lead the reader down the path you want him to take. Remember to keep it short and try to require no more than three clicks!

• If you're paying someone to help build your site, show your designer your road map to avoid costly revisions later. If you're creating your own site, you might want to create a paper version (one sheet of paper for each web page) and ask a couple of friends to see if they can follow your road map to specific destinations without getting lost.

"Been There, Done That" AUTHOR TIP ✔

"Looking for a low-cost and fast way to get your book website up and running? I have used Lunar Pages (www.lunarpages.com) LP Quicksite templates for my books. For less than $250 including one year of domain hosting, I create a custom header (with the help of my graphic designer) that can easily be placed in a custom header template. Then using their easy-to-administer website content management system, I have literally had a website up and live within a weekend! Their LP Quicksite offering gives numerous choices of templates and includes a blog, shopping cart and gallery feature. You don't need to know HTML, but if you know a little, it can be a WOW site at a WOW cost savings!"

— *Sherré L. DeMao, Author,* 50 Marketing Secrets of Growth Companies in Down Economic Times, *www.50marketingsecrets.com*

Chapter 10:

Building Your Website: Building Relationships with the Reader

As an author, you have a vested interest in turning the transaction of buying a book into an ongoing and longstanding relationship between you and the reader. Your website is one of the most important ways you can develop and nurture this relationship, but you need to understand what makes readers reach out to authors so that you can keep them coming back for more.

What Readers Really Want

When a reader finds a book that is really special, the reader wants to continue the experience. A non-fiction book may be so helpful that readers want more tips, more information, or help in applying the book's content to their own situation. A fiction book might build such a pleasant or interesting make-believe world with characters that have become real to the reader that readers don't want to leave. They want more details, inside information, and hints about what happens next.

Readers also want to feel that they have gotten to know you better as a person. Maybe they are interested in knowing why you chose to write about your topic, or how you came to be an expert. Often, they want to know what kinds of books you read, who you look up to as experts, and what you'll be doing next.

To the extent that your website can meet these needs and answer these questions, you'll be building a relationship with the people who keep you in business as an author.

What Authors Really Want

Of course, authors want people to buy and read their books. Authors also want readers and reviewers to say nice things about the book to others, encouraging more sales. Authors would like to be featured in the media as an expert and as the writer of a successful book. Some authors want to use a book to encourage readers to become clients of their business. Many authors see the value in being invited as a speaker to events, conferences and conventions. They want to use the book as a platform; and they also want to use speaking engagements to connect with more readers.

For authors who plan to write more than one book, they'll want to keep readers fired up about how much they liked Book One so that they will run out and buy Book Two. Authors who have written a book about making personal, social or political change may also want to keep readers engaged so that readers will put what they've read into action. Most authors want to be seen as experts and as successful and credible professionals.

Whether or not your website is successful depends on how well is gives readers what they want and helps you get what you want as the author.

Value Beyond the Book

Think of your book as the ice breaker for an ongoing conversation between the author and the reader. If the book has made an impact on the reader, it's only natural for him or her to want to continue the conversation, ask follow-up questions, or go deeper. That's why it's important for your site to give readers something they won't find anywhere else — extra value.

"Value" can take many different forms. You could have a forum area where readers can post questions and you can respond, or where readers can discuss the book with each other. You could post extra material that didn't fit in the book, or updated information that became available after the book went to press. You can add your voice and personality through blogging, audio and video so that readers who can't see you in person at an event still have the feeling that they've met you. Most of all, you can extend what it was that they really liked about the book by giving them more of it.

For a non-fiction author, this can include posting new tips, links to additional resources, quizzes or research results. For a fiction author, it might mean creating new content not available elsewhere, or posting content first on your own site to reward faithful readers. Authors who have a new book in the works definitely want to let readers, reporters and reviewers know, and readers who enjoyed the first book will find it valuable to know that there's more good stuff to come.

One way to provide this value is through free downloads and an email newsletter. A free download could be a bonus chapter, brand-new article or report, but anything that can be delivered via a web link or email is a possibility, so long as the reader would consider it to be valuable. If you ask visitors who want to receive the free download to enter an email address, you are now building a permission-based mailing list (otherwise known as an opt-in list).

It's important to have permission before sending out group emails (such as announcements or newsletters) because you can get in a lot of trouble if your emails aren't wanted and get reported as "spam." The Internet community takes a very dim view of unwanted emails, and if your emails generate too many complaints, you may find your site taken down or your email disabled.

When visitors choose to enter their email address in order to get a free downloadable bonus, they are giving you permission to use that email to stay in touch. You are also making an implicit promise not to bombard them with sales pitches and junk. Email announcements and newsletters should give readers the option to unsubscribe easily.

Your opt-in list is a valuable tool for staying in touch with readers, and your website helps you to build your list and deliver the downloadable bonus items. Once you have a growing opt-in list, you can use your email newsletter to remind readers of upcoming live and online events, new books, related products, classes and speaking engagements. Treat your opt-in list like a precious treasure and only send information that readers will find valuable.

✎ ASSIGNMENT 10: Using Brain Storming as an Effective Tool

• What kind of extra content could you provide that would appeal to your readers and be valuable to them? Make a list of ideas.

• What kind of free downloads could you offer to entice visitors to your website to provide you with their opt-in permission and their email address? Make another list!

• What are some other ways you can extend the value of the book for your loyal readers?

• What features could you add to your site (like a forum board, chat room, blog comment section, etc.) that would enable readers to feel like they're really connecting with you?

"Been There, Done That" AUTHOR TIP ✔

"From a promotional standpoint, a good author website is critical. Websites are prominently featured in press releases and pitching the media; and the website is one of the first things that the press examines when deciding whether to write about your book Yes, even before the book itself. It brings everything together in one space, which makes it effortless for journalists (and readers) to learn more about you."

"Make sure your credentials and background information are easy to find, and prominently feature any news clippings you have. It may be obvious, but always have links to your social media pages and to buy your book on the homepage. To really bring in traffic, publicists encourage authors to 'blog' through their website. This should be done on a consistent basis (daily, if you can). Supplement the blog with social media sites—Twitter, Facebook, and LinkedIn! Blogs and social media sites give internet-surfers a (daily) reason to keep coming back to you, giving your book even more attention!"

— *Megan Piccirillo, Newman Communications,*
www.newmancommunications.com

Chapter 11

Building Your Website: Selling Books (And Other Things) on Your Site

Authors that self-publish need to sell their books directly through the website. Authors who are published and distributed by small or large presses may not sell their own books directly, but they certainly have an incentive to make it easy for interested readers to purchase. Selling your books and related products doesn't have to be complicated. The good news is that today's programs are very easy to set up and that you also have lots of choices.

The Scoop About Online Shopping Carts

A "shopping cart" program is really an e-commerce site that allows visitors to select and pay for products or services online and which processes and tracks payment, as well as arranges for delivery. Don't let that scare you. Today's programs are very user-friendly, and are designed to be integrated into your website with minimal set up.

If you're using a template to create your website, check and see if the template includes a shopping cart. Many programs, such as Citymax.com, already have a basic shopping cart that is designed to work with the rest of your do-it-yourself site. If your template doesn't include a shopping cart or you're using a designer for a "from scratch" site, you'll probably want to check out options such as 1ShoppingCart.com, BigCommerce.com and many more. These shopping cart programs all require a monthly fee, but the price is reasonable and it's much, much cheaper that trying to build an e-commerce site for yourself.

Before you choose an online shopping cart, here are some things to think about:

» Does it work with your hosting platform and the software you're using for your website? (If you don't know, ask your designer or your web hosting site.)

» Does it take the kinds of payments you're set up to process? Online shopping carts don't take personal checks or cash. They use digital payment sources like PayPal and credit cards. PayPal.com makes it possible for you to securely accept a direct deposit payment from the buyer's bank account and to take credit cards, but only if the buyer already has a PayPal account set up.

» To accept credit cards without using PayPal, you'll need to set up a merchant account. This is the same kind of account you would need if you sold books in person or in a store. There are rules and fees involved, so be sure to read the details if this is an option you want to activate with your shopping cart. The benefit is that with a merchant account, anyone can pay you for the books as long as they have a valid credit card, making it much easier for people to buy from you.

» Can you offer coupon codes to provide special sales and discounts? How easy is this feature to use?

» Can you upload graphics (like the cover of your book) so buyers can see what you have for sale?

» Does the cart follow up on a purchase with an automatic "thank-you" email and receipt? (An automatic follow-up email is called an autoresponder.)

» Can you set up additional auto-responders to offer customers additional specials, add-ons and related products? (Research shows that someone who has just bought from you is more likely to purchase something else if asked.)

» Does the cart make it easy for you to generate end-of-year reports (helpful for taxes) and collect sales tax?

» Does the cart make it easy to provide a link to purchase by automatically generating the link code for you?
» How does the price of the shopping cart and its features compare to other shopping cart programs? (Look for reviews and comparisons online and read what users are saying about programs.)
» Check with your tax professional to make sure you understand how to track and report sales tax for your state or province.

Digital Products and Free Stuff

If you sell paperback or hardback books, you'll need to think about how you'll process purchases, which will include charging for shipping and handling and being sure that the books are packaged and shipped promptly. You may decide to do the work yourself, or hire someone to do it for you. Or, go digital. Books and products that are digital require no packaging, shipping and handling, and they provide immediate gratification for the buyer by being instantly available. (Digital books — "e-books" — still need to be designed by an experienced professional.)

Some possibilities for digital products include:
» E-books
» E-newsletter subscriptions
» Teleseminars, webinars and online coaching related to your book
» Special reports and research findings
» Audio and video related to your book
» Screen savers, mobile phone apps, games or programs related to your book

Take a hard look at how much time you will be able to devote to handling the delivery of the books and products you sell through your site, and think hard about offering digital downloads as an option for your convenience and the convenience of your readers. Remember that while you have to pay for the cost of printing and shipping paper books and products, digital downloads have a higher profit margin because there is no printing involved and there is minimal if any packaging.

Digital downloads are also great for offering free bonus items as rewards or as incentives for people to provide their opt-in emails. Not only are digital downloads free for you to provide (requiring no shipping, postage or handling), but they also can deliver themselves automatically around the clock to buyers around the world. You can offer a free sample chapter of your book, bonus material, special reports, case studies, a slide deck from a recent presentation, audio and video and deliver it via auto-responder so that the whole process is free for you, free for the visitor and completely hands-off.

Other Ways to Sell Your Stuff

Authors who aren't self-published or who work with larger publishers often do not handle book sales directly. You can steer web visitors to purchase your book from online retailers like Amazon.com or BarnesAndNoble.com by going to the author section of their sites and generating a free web link to your book. If you're working with a designer, the designer can also generate a link for you along with a thumbnail photo of the book.

You can actually make money on every sale generated by the link on your website even if the sales occur through Amazon or another online retailer by signing up for an "affiliate program." An affiliate program essentially pays you a commission (on top of your usual royalties) when you send buyers to the partner site. You can sign up directly with big retailers to be their affiliate, or you can use a one-stop site like CommissionJunction.com to centralize your affiliate relationships in one place. Just remember that you'll need to report any affiliate commissions as income when tax season rolls around!

Many shopping cart programs also make it possible for you to set other people up as your affiliates, meaning that if you sell your own books directly (not through stores), people who agree to sell your book on their website can generate a special link that will pay them a commission on every sale that comes from their site. This is a powerful incentive to get other authors, professionals in related fields, or popular websites to offer your book for sale, because they'll make a percentage every time you make a sale through their link.

Authors can also cross-promote their books with other authors who have readers with similar tastes. The benefit is that your cross-promotion partner is exposing your book (and the affiliate link for sales) to their own opt-in newsletter list and/or web traffic, and you are doing the same for them. You both stand to make some affiliate income, and you're doing readers a favor by recommending books they are likely to want. Everyone wins! (Just make sure you're tracking and reporting affiliate income and the proper sales taxes to avoid headaches at tax time.)

✎ ASSIGNMENT 11: Researching Ideas for Your Website

- Check out several online shopping cart programs, and be sure to compare features and prices. Read reviews to see how users like the programs. Narrow it down to your top two or three choices, and see which ones work best with your website.

- Start thinking about the kinds of information you will need to set up your online shopping cart: small "thumbnail" photos of the book cover, descriptions of the books, pricing and tax information, shipping and handling costs for physical products, etc.

- Explore affiliate programs for your own books and for cross-promotions, and start thinking about other sites, authors or professionals who might be open to creating a cross promotion.

"Been There, Done That" AUTHOR TIP ✔

"A short welcoming video executed well and placed on the home page of your website will do wonders for encouraging visitors to explore your site, your book and all that you have to offer. This is very similar to warmly inviting guests into your home. It serves to warm up their first encounter with you and build relationships with visitors to your site.

"Building relationships with your prospects may be viewed as your marketing message and business development effort. Once people become familiar and comfortable with you, they are more inclined to trust you and conduct business. Video is the one venue that accomplishes all of this in one fell swoop.

"In your video, briefly explain the highlights of your site and speak to why the visitor will care – what and where are the specialty pages in which they will be most interested? With a smile on your face, guide your visitor through the highlights and encourage them to contact you whether registering for your blog, emailing or with a request such as speaking at their next event. Video is a fabulous tool for authors and leads to a very Smooth Sale!"

— *Elinor Stutz is CEO of Smooth Sale, LLC, a sales training company and the author of* Hired, *and* Nice Girls DO Get the Sale: Relationship Building That Gets Results, *www.smoothsale.net*

Chapter 12:

Building Your Website: Connect With Reporters and Event Planners

Your website isn't just a great place to build relationships with readers; it's also an essential way to make connections with reporters and with the event planners who might invite you as a speaker. Making those media and speaking connections won't happen by accident, however. You'll need to plan your website with these essential audiences in mind.

Building Your News Page

Instead of making reporters hunt for what they want, why not build a specific page for them? That's the idea behind a "News" page on your website. Your News page should have its own clearly visible tab in your main navigation so that reporters (who are usually on deadline and short on time and patience) don't have to poke around looking for information.

Once you create a place for your "news" page, you need to add the kinds of information reporters want and need. Reporters will want to be able to check basic data: who, what, when, why and where. They will also want background material. Remember that most reporters are doing their very best to provide an accurate story, and you help them do this when you make the information easy for them to access.

Reporters are also open to story suggestions, assuming that the story isn't just self-promotion. You, the author, are the best person to suggest story ideas because you know the book better than anyone. By "story suggestions" I mean different angles from which a reporter might approach writing about your book. Here are several ideas to get your creativity flowing:

» **The basic angle:** Author writes book and book is now available.
» **The local angle:** Hometown author writes new/first book
» **The journey angle:** Author overcomes overwhelming circumstances to discover true purpose in life, writes book to share journey and what he/she learned
» **The change angle:** Author endures trauma, hardship or injustice and discovers a calling to rid the world of problem.
» **The hidden story angle:** Author comes up with idea for book in a quirky or unusual way, or draws on unusual personal history, genealogy, etc.
» **The whistleblower angle:** Author exposes crime, corruption or wrongdoings in business or government
» **The research/education angle:** Author performs significant research to discover startling findings that change what the public understands about how the world works.

You get the picture. In fact, as you read through the different angles (and there are many more possibilities than what are listed here), you can probably think of many books that fit the mold.

Reporters are always looking for something that is similar enough to be familiar but different enough to warrant interest. As far as they're concerned, if the similarities are to a blockbuster book, TV show or movie, all the better, so long as the new work is different enough to avoid charges of plagiarism or being derivative. When you help reporters to spot the angle, you increase the likelihood that they will do a story on your book.

Essential Elements for Your News Page

Your News page should make it very easy for a reporter to write an interesting and accurate story about you and your book, even if he or she never interviews you or can't reach you due to a last-minute deadline. To do that, your page should offer downloadable information that can be viewed online and easily printed out. Here are some components that should be a part of your News site, as well as a quick explanation of why they are important.

Fact Sheet: This document covers the basic who, what, when, where and why. It's terse and to the point. For example, it might include the date of publication, full book title, ISBN number, your full name/pen name, the publisher, a 100 word summary of the book, ordering or purchasing information (is the book available in stores or online, and is it available via Amazon or just on the author's website). Keep the questions and answers brief.

Bio: This one-page summary gives background information about you, the author. It's not a resume. Your bio should include a recent headshot professional photo, your educational credentials, highlights of your relevant professional career, awards and accomplishments (focus on those that relate to the area of expertise associated with your book), professional memberships, big-name media appearances (if any) and a smattering of personal information if you desire (married or not, number of children, pets, area of the country where you live, hobbies).

Photo: Not only should your photo be easy to see on the News page, but you should have a downloadable photo in .jpeg format so that a reporter can quickly grab a picture with acceptable resolution. Just copying a photo displayed on your website won't work; it is unlikely to have a good enough resolution to be usable. Consider having photos in several resolutions available to accommodate web or print needs.

Frequently Asked Questions (FAQ): Think of the questions you are often asked about your book, the research behind it, how you came up with the idea, etc. Do a question and answer session with yourself and include this as a page on your News site.

Testimonials/Reviews: Help reviewers see the value your readers and industry reviewers place on your book by copying quotes from reviews and testimonials. For copyright reasons, don't copy full reviews; either take a short quote or provide a link to the review site.

Recent Press Releases: Make it easy for reporters to find out the latest news about you and your book by posting the most recent press releases you've sent out on your News page.

Upcoming Events: Reporters often like to pair coverage with an event for timeliness. Put a list of your upcoming events on your News page and make sure to update it frequently.

Audio and Video: Reporters aren't the only people likely to visit your News page. Interested readers may also go looking for information, and event planners may check out the news page as well. Use web audio to record a greeting or a short reading from your book (a program like AudioAcrobat.com makes this easy). Add video clips from your recent speeches and special events by recording with a digital video camera and loading the video to YouTube, then importing the code to your website.

Wooing Event Planners to Get More Speaking Engagements

Many authors promote their books and augment their incomes through public speaking. There are clubs, associations and national organizations dedicated to just about every topic, and they welcome speakers who have a passion for their subject. This is especially true for people who have expert credentials, and as an author, you are now an expert.

Just putting up a website won't guarantee a flood of speaking engagements. You'll still have to do some research to find the organizations best suited to your topic and approach their event planner/program director to pitch yourself as a speaker. But make no mistake about it, organizations will check you out before allowing you to speak to their members, and your website is one of the first places they'll head.

Sometimes, an event planner will hear about you through the media. He or she will read an article, interview or review, or see or hear you on TV or radio. The planner is likely to request or buy a copy of your book, and then look at your website before contacting you to make sure you really would be a good match. Sometimes, planners happen upon your book and go straight from the book to your site (which is why it's so important to have your website information in the back of your book).

Regardless of how an event planner happens to come looking for you as a potential speaker, you want to make sure that he or she finds exactly what's needed to assure that you would be a great speaker. As with the News page, you'll want to make sure that your Speaker page is easy to find your main navigation, and that it has a page all to itself. Here are some other ideas of what to put on your Speaker page:

» A link to your News page with a list of resources that are available there, such as your FAQ and Fact Sheet.

» A specialized bio that emphasizes not only your author credentials, but your speaking experience and your most-requested topics. Make your topic titles engaging and be sure to include a couple of sentences for each topic emphasizing listener benefit.

» Testimonials from the event planners who have already asked you to speak, as well as from enthusiastic participants.

» Video clips from speeches you've given that show you in action and give an event planner an idea of your presentation style and how you connect with an audience.

Getting More Out of Your News and Speaking Pages

Now that you've created great News and Speaking pages, you need to let everyone know about them. One of the easiest ways to do this is to include the link directly to the News page of your site in every press release and as part of your email signature block when you contact reporters. You can also use a link directly to the Speaker page when you contact organizations to submit an application to speak, and use the link in your email signature for event-related emails.

If you create a printed speaker kit, make sure that you include the link to your Speaker page. (Note that it is a lot less expensive to direct people to your website to download your speaker materials than it is to pay for printing and postage to mail the same information.)

Use your News page and your Speaker page as a specialized electronic business card. When you post press releases to online PR sites, make sure you have the link to your News page as part of your contact information. When you approach bloggers on sites like BloggerLinkUp.com or on radio guest sites like RadioGuest-List.com, use the link to your News page to give bloggers and hosts a good idea of your media savvy and prior experience as a guest. You can use your Speaker page link on any online speaker directory site that does not require you to book through a bureau or booking agent. So if you sign up for a site like eSpeakers.com, make sure you use your Speaker page link in your contact information.

You may also decide to create specialized business cards specifically to share with reporters and event coordinators. Using an online printer like Vistaprint.com makes this a very affordable alternative. If you do create specialized cards, make sure you include a link to your News and/or Speaker page to make your web page work hard to bring you business!

✎ ASSIGNMENT 12: Writing Your First Drafts

- Create first drafts of your essential News page materials: Bio, Fact Sheet, and FAQ. Choose a professional photo, and think about how best to use audio and video. Ask several friends to proofread and comment on your materials before finalizing them.

- Create first drafts of your Speaker page materials: Bio with speaking experience, topics, recommendations, etc. Arrange to have a video made of your next speaking experience to add to your site.

"Been There, Done That" AUTHOR TIP ✔

"A functional website that is easy to navigate is important when marketing to consumers, but critical in business-to-business selling. Here you are dealing with professional buyers and they look for different information than do consumers or trade buyers. Here are some important points to consider when selling to non-bookstore buyers:

- Have a separate landing page for each segment. Corporate buyers want to know how your book can meet their needs. Buyers at associations, schools and government agencies have different needs.
- Your discount structure could be different for each segment and you do not want others seeing your pricing for all segments. Similarly, you may offer different payment options and terms.
- Offer your content for sale in different formats for business buyers. In addition to printed books and e-books you might sell booklets, DVDs, CDs or other forms.
- Offer other services as appropriate, such as consulting and speaking. These are of little interest to consumers and trade buyers.

"The testimonials you show will probably be different for each segment. Buyers may be impressed by notable figures in their industry, but perhaps not as much by unknowns (to them).

"Your bio will contain different credentials, depending on your prospective customers. As you can see, one website will not fit all your opportunities. Customize the landing pages for each potential buyer and you should see your sales increase."

— Brian Jud, author of How to Make Real Money Selling Books.
brianjud@bookmarketing.com or www.premiumbookcompany.com
twitter.com/bookmarketing

Chapter 13

Building Your Website: Sight, Sound, Motion and Social Media

You're well on your way to building a website that works hard to help you sell books and land speaking engagements. Now you have some "tools" to make your site even more appealing and encourage your viewers to stay longer on your pages. One way to do this is by learning to use audio and video to enhance your site.

Web Video Basics Make You a Star

Video production is easier than ever before, thanks to many affordable and easy-to-use digital video cameras and webcams. These cameras often have software built into them to make it very easy to download what you've shot to your computer, do basic editing, and upload to a video-sharing site like YouTube.

Video is an important addition to your website because it helps visitors feel as if they've met you in person. It can transport you from simple words on a page to being a real, live person. That helps readers, reporters and event promoters to get a better sense of the "real you."

Your public appearances can also be dramatically improved by effectively utilizing video of yourself. While it can feel awkward at first to watch yourself on video, the benefit is worth the discomfort. It's likely that you have some unconscious mannerisms, repeated phrases or awkward transitions that distract your audience and make your presentation less effective. These "distractions" will become painfully obvious when you watch the video for the first time. Without prior formal training through a program such as Toastmasters, or by working with a speaking coach, you probably have many habits or mannerisms that will need to be adjusted.

Spend time in watching your own video presentation. Take notes about what you're doing well and what could be better. Even speakers who are long-time professionals will watch videos of themselves to continually improve their presentation. It's similar to athletes who watch video of their games or matches to look for ways to improve their skills. If it's essential for the pros, it's something you should strongly consider for yourself!

On your "News," "Speaker" and other pages, video can play a very important role. Consider having a short video clip on your home page to greet visitors; or to draw them in with an exciting presentation excerpt. You can create short videos for as many of the pages in your site as you want. Here are some guidelines to keep in mind. They are based on what others have found to work well for them.

» Keep videos under five minutes long. One to three minutes is best.

» Make sure that videos load quickly and play easily. You don't want to annoy readers by freezing their computers with a slow-loading video!

» Don't include images of other people in your videos unless you have their signature on a permission slip. It's easier to ask and not need the document than to have to remove video if someone complains that their image was used without permission.

» Work with your web designer to make sure that the video plays well on a variety of computers and web browsers. One advantage to using the video embed code from a site like YouTube is that the YouTube folks have done the work to assure that the code works well.

» Think twice before having your video play automatically. There are pros and cons to auto-play. On the plus side, the immediate sound and motion may draw viewers into your site and keep them interested while the clip plays. On the down side, people browsing at work or in quiet settings may not appreciate having an unexpected voice booming through their speakers.

Audio Adds Personality and Excitement

Web audio can also add interest to your site. Programs like AudioAcrobat.com record your voice and store it in a format that is compatible with computer playback, such as MP3 (the format used for music). By using AudioAcrobat.com to record your messages, all you have to do is dial the phone; everything else is automated. The program will process your recording and format it, then provide a link for you to download the audio just like a music file. Programs like AudioAcrobat can also give you the code to embed your audio on your site, complete with a nifty set of buttons to start, stop and pause.

Audio is great for a greeting to visitors, welcoming them to your site. Authors love web audio because it makes it easy to include a link for visitors to hear you read from your new book. If you offer your book as an audiobook, you might include the web audio of a free sample chapter or two.

Some authors go a step further and begin to podcast. Podcasting is the online version of doing your own radio show. Some podcasters record with inexpensive microphones and free audio editing software like Audacity®, while others take the easy road and use AudioAcrobat, which can upload your audio directly to iTunes. Podcasters connect with listeners through sites like BlogTalkRadio.com and LibSyn.com.

If you decide to do a podcast, you'll have a lot of decisions to make, such as whether you will be the sole guest and muse about life and writing, or whether you will invite other authors or notable people to be your guests. It's possible to add your podcast to your website so that visitors to your site discover your podcast and have one more reason to check back frequently or to get to know you better.

Don't Forget Photos

Still photos might not be as exciting as video, but they can pack a punch on your site. Use a digital camera to snap photos of yourself at signings and events. Be sure to get pictures with bookstore managers, readers, celebrities and other guests. If your book tour takes you to interesting locations, throw in a few snapshots of scenery and landmarks.

There are many photo sharing sites available. Flickr.com is one of the best known, and makes it very easy to integrate your photos with all of your social media sites as well as your Website. Flickr frowns on photos that are overtly commercial, so steer clear of using the site for product shots or logos, and emphasize shots that show you interacting with other people.

A few guidelines for using photos:

» Make sure that photos catch you and everyone else in the shot in a flattering and professional light. Avoid shots where everyone is holding a beer bottle or where people look jet lagged, tired or drunk. Steer clear of shots that might be considered showing you or anyone else in a compromising or easily misunderstood setting. When in doubt, don't share the photo.

» Tag your photos to make them work harder for you with search engines. Include your name, the event/location name, and the name of other celebrities or authors in the shot. For shots with members of the general public, avoid using last names of the readers or participants in the shot with you.

» Don't use photos of children (or anyone under age 18) without written, parental permission.

Sight, Sound, Motion and Social Media

When you go to all the work to create video, audio and photos, don't stop with posting them on your website. Flickr, YouTube and AudioAcrobat also make it very easy to share with social media sites like Facebook, MySpace and your own blog. Many book/reader/author sites, such as Shelfari, GoodReads and even your own Amazon profile page, also permit some use of audio, video and photos. While you can't share the actual photo or video on Twitter, you can easily share a link to a page where your followers can see for themselves.

Having a website does NOT take away the need for you to be present on social media. And having a presence on social media doesn't get you off the hook when it comes to having an effective website. Ideally, your website is a more permanent location for readers and reporters to find you; almost like having a storefront. However, because it is sometimes difficult or expensive to make frequent changes to your website, social media puts the power in your hands to add audio, video, photos and comments as often as you wish.

Websites rely on search engines to help readers find your site, or on people knowing your domain name from your book or business card. Social media enables you to find where readers are already gathering and invite them to be your friend or follower. Social media sites also encourage a two-way conversation between author and reader, where websites tend to be less interactive.

You can get double duty out of the time you spend blogging and commenting on Facebook and Twitter by having your social media pages automatically update your website. Use Really Simple Syndication (RSS) (which is built into all social media sites) to feed your social media updates right onto your web page to keep your content fresh.

When you create a web page that incorporates video, audio, photos and social media, you will move away from only having page after page of boring text. You and your book will seem to come to life. You can reach out to make contact with readers, reviewers and reporters. Visitors glimpse your personality and unique style, which may encourage an invitation to speak or do a signing. Experiment and see how it brings your site to life!

✎ ASSIGNMENT 13: Brainstorming for Video Ideas

• What are you already doing that lends itself to web video or digital online photos? If you don't already own a digital video camera and a digital still camera, check out the prices and options. Make a list of all the ways you could use video, audio and photos on your site.

• If you're already on Facebook, Twitter and other social media sites, think of how you might want to get twice the value for your time by having the social media sites update your Web page. If you're not on social media, check out Facebook, Twitter, YouTube, and Flickr and see how other authors are using social media to enhance their outreach.

"Been There, Done That" AUTHOR TIP ✔

"I cannot emphasize enough how important self-promotion is for the modern author. Not all publishers have vast marketing budgets to lavish on a title, and anything the author can do to get their voice heard is going to help sell copies of their work. The most important tool for the author in all of this is undoubtedly a good personal website, whether this is a simple blog, or something more lavish. It's easy enough now, and pretty cheap, to get a blog or website up and running.

"You need not be afeared of new technology. It's also one of the quickest and most direct ways of reaching your audience, whether that is your thoughts on life or news on your latest release or work-in-progress. My tip would be, though, to make your website look nice and professional. Publishers and editors have the Internet too, and anything that makes their lives easier to spot you amongst the crowd is going to be a big help to you. Keep it simple but stylish. Don't crowd your site with endless images of every single edition of your novel in all its twenty-one translations. Instead, tell us who you are, what your works are and why we should be excited about what you're producing. Get this right and watch that hit counter rise!"

— Jonathan Oliver is the Editor-in-Chief of Solaris and Abadddon Books, his first novel was Twilight of Kerberos: The Call of Kerberos *and he has also edited a collection of horror stories set on the Underground called* The End of The Line.

www.solarisbooks.com, www.abaddonbooks.com

Chapter 14

Promoting Your Website: SEO, RSS and Other Important Add-Ins

When you're learning your way around the Internet, there are a lot of abbreviations. "URL" is short for Uniform Resource Locator — otherwise known as your domain name. "WWW" of course stands for World Wide Web. But how about other terms like SEO or RSS? In this chapter, you'll learn more about SEO and RSS and discover why both are important for great author websites.

SEO Makes Your Site Easy to Find

"SEO" stands for Search Engine Optimization. SEO helps your website get noticed by search engines, like Google, to make it easier for interested people to find your site. SEO is really important because it connects your site to topic words (called "keywords') that a person might use to search for information on a topic when he or she doesn't know a book, author, expert or site to look for specifically. Having "good SEO" enables people to find you online more easily and to buy your book, even if they don't know anything about you.

SEO can get pretty complicated because it's all about making sure that the complex algorithms that Google (and other search engines) use to quickly index millions of web pages will find your page and consider it relevant. You don't have to worry about the complicated stuff right now.

The most important thing to remember is that when a person types in a query on a search engine, he or she will often use topical words. These could include words such as "diet," "cocker spaniels," "cherry pie recipe" or "parenting tips," rather than the name of an author or the title of a book.

Search engines have powerful secret computer code that immediately runs out and searches every page on the Internet looking for websites that appear to be "relevant" to the query typed by the user. Each search engine has its own algorithms to determine "relevancy." It also helps to eliminate sites that may mention one of the words in the search terms but which aren't really about that search term.

It's all about context and how often the search terms (keywords) are used. So a blogger who mentions "I'm on a diet" wouldn't rate as being highly relevant with a search for "diets." However, a site about a diet book or a diet program would be rated much more relevant.

The trick is to understand search engines well enough to help your pages be as relevant as possible on the keywords that readers who need your information (but don't yet know about your book) would be most likely to use. You can do this in several ways:

» Go to Google Keyword Tool (it's free) and see how some of the words you use most to talk about your subject and book rank in terms of the number of times people use them in search queries. You'll find that two synonymous words often have very different rankings, with one word being used millions of times and the other only a few thousand times. Always choose the more frequently-searched word over less popular words when you write headlines and web copy to help your page show up in as many results as possible.

» Make sure that the name of your book and your name appear in text and not just as part of photos or graphics on your site. Search engines read text but can't read images in photos or graphics. So if the only mention of your book's title is in a photo of the cover, search engines won't see the title on your page.

» Whenever you add photos, video or audio, "tag" the item with descriptive titles and keywords to help search engines recognize relevant material.

» Whenever you're given a chance to add keywords or tags to blog posts, videos, or web pages, do it! Use the words that best relate to your topic and book title, your industry, your area of expertise and of course, your own name.

» Include a link to your home page in online press releases, comments that you post to blogs and forum boards, and in any social media posts. Search engines factor in the number of times other relevant sites link to your page as an indication of your site's popularity and importance.

» Once you've found the most frequently searched keywords that relate to your book and topic, use those words and phrases as frequently as possible in your web copy. At the same time, remember that human beings are also going to read your site, so don't make the text sound stilted or strange just to please the search engines. Strike a balance to serve both audiences.

» When you post an online press release, be sure to use the most frequently searched keywords that are relevant in your headline to have your release show up as often as possible.

» Search engines like sites that are frequently updated, and tend to ignore sites that don't get regular updates. An easy way to get a supply of new content onto your site without having to upload it yourself is to use RSS to feed your new Facebook, blog and Twitter posts directly onto pages of your website.

SEO is constantly changing because Google and the other search engines refine their algorithms frequently. Some people believe that the search engines also change their search technology to keep too many people from figuring out their secrets and gaming the system to get to the top of the rankings.

The bottom line is that there will always be ways that you or your web designer can tweak your site for better SEO. You should never consider SEO to be completely finished. On the other hand, it's amazing how many authors and businesses never even think to optimize their pages in order to rank better in searches. This is like turning off all the lights in your store, and then waiting for customers to come in!

What about RSS?

"RSS" stands for Really Simple Syndication. RSS is Web code that enables you to post information in one place (such as on your blog) and have it automatically update somewhere else (such as on your website or Facebook page). RSS comes in handy because it means that instead of having to cut and paste the same information in several places, computer code will make sure it all happens automatically.

Look at your blog and social media pages, and you may see a little icon that looks like a dot with three concentric arcs (usually the icon is orange). Click on the icon, and you'll get the RSS code to help you subscribe to the site. A subscription means that whenever updates are posted, subscribers will receive the new information automatically, so they don't have to remember to go out and check.

Wouldn't you like to build your blog readership by having readers subscribe so they don't have to think about checking for new posts? And wouldn't it be great to enable reporters to subscribe to your News page so that they would automatically get updated information on new events or publications? RSS makes that easy.

To generate an RSS link for pages on your website, your best bet is to work with a web designer who understands the code. But on social media, RSS is very easy to use. That's because social media sites were built with RSS in mind. In fact, every time you see one of the little icons to "connect" to Twitter, Facebook, LinkedIn or other social media sites, you're using RSS.

Do you want to have your blog automatically update your Facebook page? Go to your Notes tab on your Facebook page and use the Import Settings button. This will ask you for the RSS code for the site you would like to have automatically update your page. Use the RSS code generated by your blog to link your blog to your Facebook page. If you don't want to link your blog, you might want to link your Twitter or Flickr accounts.

You'll also find RSS on author/book sites like Shelfari, BookMarketing.ning and GoodReads. Some of these sites allow you to use RSS to import content from outside the site onto your profile page, and some of the sites let you use RSS to take content from their site and feed it to other sites. Once you know what RSS is, you can begin to think of how best it can help you get the most out of your online posting time.

When to Hire a Pro

To go much beyond the basics covered here, you will probably want to consult a web designer or SEO professional. Not only do the search engines continually change their SEO criteria, but it can become very time consuming to make the constant tweaks necessary to stay at the tip-top of the search engine results.

E-commerce companies have a business need to invest time and money into the latest and greatest SEO. Those companies make a never-ending investment because they depend on search results for their full income. This level of SEO investment can get very expensive very quickly. Fortunately, most authors don't need to be quite that SEO-intensive. Once you put the basics in place, remember to update your keywords whenever you release a new book or add a new topic to your writing.

If just thinking about SEO makes your eyes glaze over or if you truly don't have the time, ask your Web designer for help. Get an estimate on a basic, intermediate and "the works" level of SEO, and invest what you can to make your site as visible as possible. Be sure to remember to budget for updates to your SEO once or twice a year.

Two other free programs can help you see where your site is doing well attracting visitors and where it could use some help. Google Analytics (www.google.com/analytics/) is great for tracking spikes in traffic and seeing which search terms and outside sites are sending the most visitors to your site. You can use Google Analytics to track the traffic after a big online promotion or book tour to see how much traffic your efforts generated.

WebsiteGrader.com is another great site to get a free analysis of how your current SEO is working and where you could use some help. You enter your home page address and Website-Grader generates a report to suggest opportunities for SEO improvement. It can be helpful to send the report to your web designer or SEO professional as a starting point in your conversation. Be sure to get an estimate before beginning any SEO work, as it can be expensive.

✎ ASSIGNMENT 14: Using SEO to Help Your Website

• If you already have a website, run WebsiteGrader.com for ideas of how to improve your SEO.

• If you don't yet have a site or are just building one, make sure to look up your best keywords on Google Keyword Tool, and then use them frequently in your web copy and tags. Sign up for Google Analytics as soon as your site goes live.

"Been There, Done That" AUTHOR TIP ✔

"As a publisher I teach my authors to think of their website as a multi-media channel on the Internet, much like a cable TV and radio broadcast where they are the star. Be creative and fun — your website is only limited by your imagination. Create a site that downloads quickly and thanks visitors with a free short story. Show off your talent with excerpts from your novels, MP3 readings, MP4 (video) clips of talks at book signing events or a host a show. Provide a press kit and keep a calendar of live events updated so that fans can meet you. Offer your books as autographed copies through your own bookstore.'

"By far the most important function of an author website is building a database of your fans' email addresses. Offer them free opt-in email updates in exchange for their email address and promise them you will not share that address with anyone. This is where you embrace the interactivity of the Internet and reach out to your fans on a monthly basis. Your goal is to build a fan base of 10,000 people that will subscribe to you directly. Provide exclusive first viewings of short stories and/or serialized novels that you email directly to your subscribers twelve times a year. Charge $19 to $29 per year to subscribe and you will earn an income of $190,000 to $290,000 on top of your work for publishers. The author with the biggest database wins!"

— *Bruce Gehweiler, Publisher Marietta Publishing and co-author of* Breaking into Fiction Writing! *with C.J. Henderson*

Chapter 15

Promoting Your Website: Drive Traffic to Your Site and Readers to Your Book

Congratulations! You've created your website and launched it online. But you're not finished yet. Building your website is only the first step. For your site to engage readers, sell books, woo reviewers and impress reporters, they need to know that the site exists. They need a reason to come back to your site time and again. And they need to find interesting, engaging content that will want to make them read more. Part of promoting your book is also promoting your website, which becomes your 24/7 book event.

The Basics of Website Promotion

Some of the best promotion tactics are the most basic. Make sure that your website is printed on everything — and I do mean everything. Ask your publisher to put the website address in the back pages of your book — and include an invitation for readers to visit with a promise of what kind of content and interaction they will find when they come. Add your web address to your business card and to any promotional materials you create for your book. This includes bookmarks, book-specific business cards, posters, signage, banners, and one-sheet flyers.

Your web address also belongs in your email signature. Below your name, include "Author, (Your book title here)" and on the next line, your book web address. If you also have a business web address, it's OK to use both. Your email signature not only promotes your website with every email that you send, but you can use that signature block when you comment on blogs and in forums, letting readers know where they can reach you if they've enjoyed your input.

If you do a newsletter related to your book, a blog, or any social media sites like a Facebook or Twitter page, make sure your book website is prominently positioned so that readers can find out more about your book and about you, the author.

If you've written a non-fiction book that relates to your business, don't be afraid to mention the book title and website on your business site and in your business mailings. That can include your business newsletter, signage, brochures, flyers, invoices, statements and any other communication you create to your prospects, vendors and customers.

Make sure that you reference your book title and book website in your online profile for any membership communities, clubs, associations and directories in which you take part. So many people overlook the valuable online real estate in the free profiles they receive with membership to all kinds of organizations, from the Chamber of Commerce to their trade or industry association, to their hobby or cultural groups. Don't be shy! Many of these profile sites allow for more than one website in recognition that members may more than one business-related web address. Take advantage of the visibility and make sure that your site is easy to find.

This is especially true for the profile related to your LinkedIn page, your blog, your Facebook or Twitter profile, or any other social media sites where you are active. Letting people know about your book and how to read more about the book is another way they can get to know you. It's an important and legitimate part of who you are.

Taking the Next Step in Promoting Your Site

Promoting yourself as an author is part of promoting your book. (For tips on how to promote yourself and your book in the first year of publication, see *The Thrifty Author's Guide to Launching Your Book Without Losing Your Mind.*) And an important part of promoting both yourself and your book lies in promoting your website.

As an author, you are automatically an expert. Why? Because you wrote a book! If you've written non-fiction, your expertise is focused on the subject of your book, your research, any professional credentials related to your book, and any work experience that contributed to the book or that extends from the book. So, if you wrote a book on financial planning based on a 20-year career as a financial advisor, having an MBA in finance, and the experiences of the hundreds of clients you've served, all of those things make you an expert.

Fiction authors are also experts. You may have a degree or years of research invested in your topic. It doesn't matter whether that topic is medieval warfare, shipwrecks, pirates or ancient Greek mythology, what counts is that you know more about your subject than the average person. You have also successfully navigated the publication maze, whether you are self-published or traditionally published. That also makes you an expert on writing a book, writing a book in your particular genre, and other aspects of the writing life.

Promote your expert status, yourself and your book — along with your website. One way to do this is to write articles related to the topic of your book and post them on article directory sites like eZineArticles.com. Article directory sites let others use your article for free in newsletters and on blogs but only if they reprint it word-for-word and give you full attribution. Attribution includes your name, book title and website.

You can also get visibility on sites that match would-be guests with bloggers and radio shows. For example, sites like BloggerLinkUp.com, MyBlogGuest.com and RadioGuestList.com let experts with information to share post a willingness to be a guest, and allow bloggers and radio hosts who need guests to post their requirements. Of course every guest blog or radio interview should include mentions of your website. This should be true of any media coverage you receive and any press release you send out. Always include your website and let people know what great content is waiting for them.

You can also use social bookmarking to promote your site. Social bookmarking is the online equivalent of putting a sticky note on a favorite article with a 'read this' message, only it's posted on the Internet instead of the office bulletin board. Sites like StumbleUpon, Digg, and Delicious all provide ways to share content you've found to be interesting with the rest of the world. You can encourage other people to share your content by using AddThis.com to put the icons of the major social media networks right at the top of your page so that readers can indicate their interest with a single click.

For a very small investment, you can also create a Facebook ad for your book. You define the audience profile that will get to see your ad. You also define your monthly and lifetime campaign budget, so there are no expensive surprises. This can be another great way to promote your book and encourage readers to find both your Facebook page and your website.

Don't forget to ask your publisher to help you promote your website. Make sure that any author profile or catalog copy includes your website if at all possible. If you are self-published, your distributor may have a catalog of titles with brief descriptions, and your book's description should include your site. If you work with a special sales organization like BookMarketingWorks.com, let the sales force and the catalog folks know about your site.

If you find other associations dedicated to your topic, or other clubs or organizations of writers in your genre, write a brief personal note of introduction and let them know about your availability as a speaker and blogger, and include your website. Tell them what kind of content they'll find on the site, and give them a good reason to visit.

Create a Reason to Linger and Return

Promoting your website is only part of the picture. For the website to do your book any good, you need to have interesting content on the site. Content should not just be a sales pitch. To be effective, your web content should offer real value and real solutions for the reader. You can make your website more attractive for readers so that they spend more time on the site and come back more often by offering content they can't find anywhere else. This can include free excerpts, articles related to your topic, quizzes, surveys, research, case studies, and other bonus extras.

At speaking events where you are a presenter, give the audience a reason to visit your site to receive the notes or slide show from the speech, a related checklist or article, or other value-added resources. Train your readers (through your newsletters, blog posts and in-person appearances) to visit your website for content they can only get from you. This can include a sneak peek of the next book, short stories set in your world or articles about your subject, upcoming event calendars, contests and other fun and useful information.

Even a great website needs promotion in order to be discovered. Once you've made your website the best that it can be, help it become a sales engine for your book by making sure everyone knows about your site.

✎ ASSIGNMENT 15: Cross-Promoting Your Website

- Make a list of all the places where you can add your website or promote it on your materials.

- Brainstorm to create appealing content and downloadable extras (like articles or excerpts) you can add to keep your site fresh and exciting.

"Been There, Done That" AUTHOR TIP ✔

"I've seen quite a few Websites created by book authors, and many fall short. Here's why: The information explains the author's books, but the wording often fails to persuade readers to purchase those books. Let's face it; most creative writers are not experienced advertising copywriters.

Tip One: Hire a professional advertising copywriter to compose the sales portion of your site. Here's the next issue I see that makes visitors not want to buy books from a website: Any error in the copy makes visitors assume the books are unedited, too, whether true or not.

Tip Two: Hire a professional editor to read all the copy to ensure it is error free, clear to readers, and compelling to buyers. Do this before the web pages are designed. You'd be surprised how many gremlins creep into copy during the design phase, but you've read the copy too many times by that point and can no longer spot errors. You need one final helper.

Tip Three: Have a professional proofread the final version, with all the design elements in place, before the site is posted for public viewing. Yes, professionals cost money, but a little currency spent making your website its best will be returned to you many times in higher book sales."

—Bobbie Christmas, Zebra Communications — editing that improves book-length manuscripts, marketing materials, and websites www.zebraeditor.com

Chapter 16:

Promoting Your Website: Tying Your Site to Your Marketing Program

While your website is an important part of your promotional strategy, it shouldn't be the only marketing for your book. Marketing works best when many different approaches are tied together with a common theme. Your website can be the common point of reference that anchors all your other activity, creating a place where readers, reporters, reviewers and event coordinators go to find current and correct information.

Tying It All Together

Your website can be the central point from which a visitor gets the big picture about you and your book. In order for this to happen, you'll need to build your marketing efforts with your website in mind, and make sure that your web updates and development tie into all your other marketing activities.

For example, make sure that your website lets visitors know your upcoming schedule for speaking events, book signings, conference appearances, seminars and any other events related to your book. Whenever the events are free, don't forget to let visitors know the details so they can easily participate. If the events require a fee, such as a seminar based on your book, your website can be your 24/7 sales pro, taking orders and enabling quick-and-easy sign-up.

You already know how important it is for all of your marketing materials to reference your website. But it's also important for visitors to your website to know where to find the specials you offer in ads, direct mail and social media. If you're offering a discount with a coupon, let visitors to your website know where to find the coupon. If they can get a special offer via direct mail or email, give them a way to sign up to receive the mailing. Not only do you add to your opt-in mailing list, but you make your visitor happy about getting a deal.

If you're offering special content on your social media sites, make sure your web visitors have a link where they can click to participate. And of course, if you've recently been featured in print or on radio or TV, include a link to share the article or interview whenever possible.

Remember that your website is a multimedia experience, so make sure to include video from your speaking engagements, audio clips from recent teleseminars, or links to download bonus extras. You can also offer web-only special offers, where visitors to your website get extra items, discount pricing, unique product bundles or other attractive incentives that are not available elsewhere. Make sure to promote your web-only offers through your newsletter, social media and other marketing, and change your offers fairly frequently to keep visitors coming back for more. Always strive to provide more than the visitor expects to delight and surprise.

Extend and Amplify with Your Website

A live speaking engagement, special event or book signing lasts for a finite amount of time. But on the web, you can extend the life of your special events indefinitely. Your website becomes a way to amplify the impact of your promotional events and make them last longer, extending their value to you and to the customer.

For example, you may give a speaking engagement that only lasts for half an hour. But if you encourage listeners to visit your website, you can extend the amount of interaction you have with them. Give them a chance to download the slides or program notes, read an article you've written, listen to an interview, or get a special discount on a seminar or webinar based on your book. When you encourage people who attend your live events to sign up for downloadable freebies on your website, you gain their opt-in permission to stay in touch with them through your newsletter and email. That extends your relationship with them indefinitely.

If you hold a special event like a workshop or seminar related to your book, think of ways to use your website to extend and amplify the program. For example, you might offer a free email mini-program via auto-responder, where people who attend your program can sign up to receive additional content not covered in your presentation via email.

You can post photos and video from the event, including videotaped testimonials from participants. Use your blog to continue the conversation about your speaking topic or the event theme, so that the dialogue goes on long after the event is over. Offer people the opportunity to buy admission to the next event at a discount, or provide the chance to purchase a next-step program that builds on what you covered in the first event.

You won't be able to visit everyone's local bookstore, but you can provide a free download of a signed bookplate or a poster with quotations taken from your book. Offering these kinds of items makes a personal connection with readers and lets them know that you care about them even if you never have the chance to meet in person.

Of course, your website is also a great place to promote upcoming appearances, events, seminars, signings and live interviews. Encourage your website visitors to come out and see you in person whenever possible. Not only does this strengthen your connection to the reader, but by increasing the number of people in your live event audience, you convince event coordinators that you are the kind of expert they want for a repeat performance.

When you share a stage with other authors or experts or when someone is kind enough to mention your name in a review, article or blog post, promote the people who promote you by sharing links to their blog or site. Not only is this a gracious way to say 'thank you,' but it also helps your site in the search engine rankings, since your site will show up whenever anyone searches for the names of the people you've mentioned.

Get Your Readers Involved

Most people are naturally helpful, especially when it involves something they like. Appeal to the site visitors who have read your book and liked it by asking them to forward your newsletter, email their friends, bookmark your web page on sites like StumbleUpon or Digg, or 'like' your Facebook page.

Having the AddThis.com social media buttons on every page of your site makes it easy for visitors to share the content they find useful with all their social media friends. Ask your readers to recommend your book and site to their book clubs, libraries and professional associations. It's amazing what happens when you just ask people to help!

When you make your website a natural part of all your promotional activities, your entire marketing effort becomes stronger and provides longer-lasting results. You also create marketing programs that create value for readers as well as sales for your book. It's a great win-win situation.

✎ ASSIGNMENT 16:

- Make a list of all the marketing you are doing for your book: newsletter, events, speaking, conferences, signings, etc. Now, think about how you might add reader value by tying in your website to amplify and extend the event experience.

- Every time you add a new marketing activity to promote your book, look for ways to add value by tying in your website for bonus items, online specials and web-only discounts.

"Been There, Done That" AUTHOR TIP ✔

"If you're an author, why build a website? Well simply put, it's your calling card. The place you want people to come to read your excerpts, to interact with you, and to build your credibility. But not just any website. You want it to reflect you. Your voice, your spirit, your message.

"You've just spent months, maybe even years, to write and develop your book. Bookstores unfortunately, are turning into dodos, and Amazon rules the waves! That means it's up to you to drive traffic to your book. But it's not enough just to have a website, you have to do what you can to make sure people visit. You need to start connecting to other blogs and websites to raise your visibility. Write articles, discuss your book, share the content, comment on other people's books, blogs and build your network of other writers and readers.

"Selling books is a business. Your business is to make sure you reach out to as many people as possible so they know you exist. When people come to your site, get them to opt-in and subscribe to your list. In return give them an excerpt from your book, or some other content that is perceived as value.'

"There are millions of online resources and websites dedicated to writers. Seek them out and emulate the author websites you admire. Successful authors carefully and strategically build their campaign for exposure. That's why having a website is essential to success."

— *Jacqueline Wales, Author of* The Fearless Factor *and* When The Crow Sings. *www.thefearlessfactor.com*

Chapter 17

Maximizing Your Website: Cross-Marketing, Collaboration and Affiliates

Marketing your book and your book website may seem overwhelming at first. But the good news is, you don't have to do it alone. Collaborating with other authors who reach a similar target reader with different content can make it much easier and more enjoyable to spread the word about your book and website. Partnering with others just makes sense, because everyone is limited in time, money and know-how. By working with other authors, you can double your exposure without adding to your cost.

The Magic of Collaboration

Avid readers may easily consume over 200 books a year. Many business people pride themselves on reading at least one business book a week, while genre readers often consume books by the bagful. So there's no reason to fear that if you collaborate with another author you will somehow lose out on a sale or a reader.

People who buy your book will also buy another dozens or even hundreds of books this year. That is true of the people who buy other authors' books as well. When you collaborate with an author who has a message of value to your target readers, you gain exposure to that author's readers, just as he or she gains exposure to your readers. And the reader benefits by getting to discover a great new author. Everyone wins.

Now that your book is published, you're likely to attend plenty of events where other authors are present. Make it a point to meet these authors and get to know them. Look for authors who are also just starting out, and target authors who would be of interest to your readership without providing a subject that directly competes with yours. For example, if you write about financial planning for small business, look for authors who write on non-financial topics that are also of interest for entrepreneurs, or on non-competing financial topics such as accounting, payroll or other services you don't offer.

Approach other authors with a win-win proposition. Point out to them that you both reach the same audience in non-competing ways, and that by collaborating, you could both double your marketing reach. You could offer to feature them on your blog or podcast, or to mention their book (make sure to read it first) in your newsletter. If you hit it off, you might consider offering joint seminars, splitting the cost of a dealer table at an upcoming event, or sharing hotel costs. Make sure to do your homework about your potential partners to be certain that their product is of professional quality and that they have a good reputation.

Collaboration means working together with another author. Cross-marketing is the process by which you introduce their books to your readers, and they introduce your book to their readers. This might involve swapping articles, blog posts or audio clips to be featured in the other person's newsletter or on their website. It could include offering one of their free download items as a thank-you bonus to people who buy your book and vice versa. It could also mean jointly hosting a special event or seminar and promoting it to both of your opt-in lists and through both websites.

Cross-marketing and collaboration are fantastic ways to promote your book because many activities are free. If you have five thousand people on your list and you cross promote with another author who also has five-thousand opt-ins on his list, you have now doubled your reach without adding anything to your cost.

Just remember to be selective with your partners. After all, you have invested a lot in gaining the trust of your readers, so your recommendation comes as the suggestion of a valued friend. Don't disappoint readers by recommending poor quality merchandise.

One key to successful collaboration and cross-marketing is to start slow. Offer an opportunity for the other author to do a guest post on your blog. Mention the upcoming guest appearance on your website and in your publicity. A good partner will make a reciprocal offer of equal value. If this small step works out, try swapping newsletter articles or doing a joint free teleseminar.

Remember to promote everything through your website and check to see if your partner is holding up his end by promoting on his site. Good partners strive to provide equal value and don't take advantage of each other. If the partnership seems to be lopsided, finish your original commitment and stop. There are plenty of good partners out there; don't work with anyone who isn't a good fit.

Collaboration and cross-marketing doesn't have to be limited to other authors. You may find that there are companies whose products or services are a natural fit for your target audience. They may see benefit in your book if it helps their prospects and customers see the value and get more from their product. Clubs, associations, professional organizations and even schools may also be a good fit. Don't be afraid to approach good partners and start a conversation.

Offering a newsletter article swap or a guest blog post is a safe, low-risk first step. Of course, be sure to feature the new article or post on your website for maximum visibility. You may even decide to swap web links and mention each other's sites on your own sites. This can be great for search engine visibility because search engines prize qualified inbound links (meaning links to your site from other credible, related sites).

When you create collaborative relationships and begin to cross-market, your goal should be to provide valuable resources to your readers, not just to sell books. Never compromise quality or integrity just to sell a few books. Your reputation is the key to your long-term success as an author, and once it has been compromised, it's very difficult to win back readers' trust. That's why it's so important to guard your opt-in list like gold.

It's OK for you to promote someone else's product to your own list, but never share your list with anyone else and absolutely never sell your list. Readers choose to share their contact information with you, but they also trust you to keep it private. Not only do you breech that trust, but a growing number of anti-spam laws are taking an increasingly harsh view of sending out unsolicited emails.

When you share or sell your list (or even worse, when you attempt to use a list someone has shared or sold to you), the people on the list are receiving emails they did not ask to receive. Your permission to email to your opt-in list is specific to you; it cannot be sold or transferred without the permission of each individual on your list.

Make sure that you stay on the right side of your subscribers by safeguarding your mailing list. And make sure that you are constantly adding to your opt-in list by having a prominent free bonus offer on every page of your website to entice visitors to give you permission to add them to your list.

A Word About Affiliates

Affiliate marketing refers to the practice of paying other people a commission to sell and promote your books, products and services for you on their websites and through their opt-in email lists. Many e-commerce and online shopping cart sites make it easy to set up affiliate commissions and offer special links to your affiliates so they can get credit for the sales they generate.

While you certainly may create an affiliate relationship with the authors and companies with whom you cross-market and collaborate, most affiliates will be people you may have never met but who think your book is a good fit for their audience. Some people make a business out of being a professional affiliate, retailing products through their site on which they make a commission for sales.

Some of the best affiliates will come from your own opt-in list, readers and customers who have experienced the value of your book first-hand and who already feel that they know you through your website, emails and promotions. With these affiliates, the commission they earn is a 'thank you' for the honor they do you by referring your book to their readers and web visitors.

If you decide to jump into affiliate marketing, investigate sites like CommissionJunction.com that make it easy for people who want to be affiliates to find quality products, like your book. Mention on your website and in your newsletter than you have an affiliate program, and provide a link for interested visitors to sign up. Make sure that you understand the tax ramifications regarding sales tax and income reporting. These requirements vary from state to state, so it's a good thing to discuss with your tax professional.

Many online book retailers, such as Amazon and Barnes and Noble also offer affiliate marketing. You can post a "buy now" link to your book on your website and direct the sales through Amazon, Barnes and Noble and other retailers if you don't handle your book's distribution. This is especially nice for people who work with traditional publishers, because they don't have the inventory of books that self-published authors have.

By using an affiliate link, not only are you making it easy for visitors to your website to order your book right away, but as an affiliate, you make an extra percentage on every sale of your own book (in addition to any royalties). Always check the laws in your state or province, since many locales have begun requiring affiliate sellers to report sales tax on Internet-based sales and of course, the money generated by your affiliate commission should be included with your taxable income. Check with your tax preparer to make sure you stay on the right side of the law.

Collaboration, cross-marketing and affiliate marketing can be great ways to leverage your website and your opt-in mailing list to promote your book to a wider audience without incurring higher marketing costs. Opportunities are all around you; you're only limited by your imagination.

✎ ASSIGNMENT 17: Brainstorming Collaboration Ideas

• Identify ten other authors or companies that might be good collaborative partners. (Hint: start small until you get comfortable with the process.) Think about what win-win offer you might make to gain their partnership, then take the plunge and connect.

• Investigate the affiliate marketing opportunities for your book and check out what kinds of affiliate options are provided by your online shopping cart software.

"Been There, Done That" AUTHOR TIP ✔

"Think of your website as the first line of defense or rather the first place a perspective reader or longtime fan will look for information about yourself or your titles. Try to tailor the information to your audience, keep it fresh. Your fans will also want to know about you as a person. You don't have to get personal. Try giving them some clues into your life that helps them to connect with you. This is what you want, a personal connection to you and your work. Also, photos of yourself at public events such as book signings or conferences will help to create that connection.

The ultimate goal is to create a base of fans or readers that will be loyal to you and your work. In this way it doesn't matter what you write or who you publish with. Your fans will seek you out no matter where you are."

—Deron Douglas, Publisher, Double Dragon Publishing Inc.

Chapter 18

Maximizing Your Website: Keep it Fresh and Sticky

You've got your website up and running. How do you encourage people to visit and keep coming back? Building web traffic has a lot to do with three factors: "freshness," "stickiness" and "bounce."

Keeping It Fresh

"Freshness" on the Internet means how recently your website was updated. We've all visited websites that are badly out of date. As a consumer, what is your impression when you visit a site that hasn't been updated in a long time and has old information? It's fair to assume that customers will wonder whether or not the company behind the website is still in business. They may also wonder if the company has shifted priorities, since keeping the website updated obviously isn't important to the owner.

Such doubts are reasonable, but damaging. They're not the kind of things you want visitors to your site thinking about you. What kind of an impression do you want? In addition to being welcoming, easy to read and simple to navigate, your website should focus on immediate consumer benefit. It should also offer new information on a regular and frequent basis, making it obvious that the site (and your company) is vibrant and dynamic.

Not only do consumers value freshness, but search engines like it, too. Search engines look for freshness and relevancy to determine which sites end up on the first page of results. Sites that haven't been updated in months (or years) just aren't deemed to be as relevant as sites that get new material on a regular basis. Stale sites fall to the bottom of the results list, a bad thing considering that most searchers rarely go deeper than the first page of results.

At this point, many business owners cringe, thinking about all the other items on their task lists and wondering how they'll fit frequent web updates onto the agenda. The good news is that it isn't nearly as difficult to keep a site fresh as it is to build it. It's also good to realize that you don't have to be the one to make updates, and a well-built modern site shouldn't require that all changes be done by a pricy web designer.

One way to update your site is to use a Wordpress-based page that is essentially a glorified blog. Since blogs are extremely easy for anyone familiar with word processing to update, you or someone on your staff can cut and paste new information, updating the page in minutes. Many people delegate the process of doing physical updates to a staffer or virtual assistant (you'll still need to determine what the new content should be, and probably write it).

RSS (Really Simple Syndication) is another way to keep your site fresh without having to lift a finger. RSS takes a frequently updated social media site (like your blog or Facebook page) and feeds the information into another site (like your web page or other social media pages). You update one site, and it feeds fresh content to several other sites automatically.

Many blogs and template programs have a built-in RSS application; if yours doesn't, it's something your web designer can easily add. Not only does RSS make it easy to keep multiple sites fresh, but it also ensures that your information is consistently fresh across your online platform.

There are many ways to keep your site fresh and maintain viewer interest. Promote and hold online events, such as readings, Q&A sessions, interviews, or radio/podcast broadcasts and invite viewers to join in from your home page. Follow up on your live signings and appearances by posting photos, audio and video shortly after the event to give web visitors a great virtual almost-like-being-there experience.

You can also create web-only specials and downloads that require your readers to visit your site on a regular basis to get new articles, short stories, and special discounts. Creating and promoting web-only content is a great way to reward visitors for returning frequently.

There's also a housekeeping aspect to freshness. It's easy to focus so much on homepage content that you forget about your photo and bio. I've seen many websites where the photo and bio are badly out of date. When your bio is outdated, you're missing out on getting credit for new books, recent events, awards or interviews. An outdated photo makes it difficult for readers to recognize you at live events, and can give the impression that your insights are also not up-to-date. Your photo and bio are ways to make a great first impression. Make sure they show you at your very best.

Internal links that work are also essential for a fresh web page. Visitors become easily frustrated when links on a page don't work, go to "page not found" messages or deliver the wrong content. Frustrated visitors are unlikely to return, and they may tell their friends about their negative experience. Since the Internet is always changing, make it a monthly ritual to check (or have someone else check) all the links on your site to assure they are helping visitors reach the intended destination.

Sticky Is Good

"Stickiness" means the length of time visitors spend on your website. The stickier a site is, the longer visitors spend exploring, watching videos, listening to audios, and reading content. It's the difference between someone who rings your doorbell and someone who comes in for coffee or stays for dinner. You not only want your site to be fresh and inviting, but you want the content to engage the visitor so that he or she has a pleasant and beneficial experience.

The key to sticky content is to make it benefit-oriented and relevant to the reader. Content should focus on what the reader wants or needs, not what you, the owner of the page, want to sell.

If your book is non-fiction, focus your content on the solution your book provides. If your book is fiction, engage your reader and draw him into your world. At a minimum, you want readers to spend time on your home page, but the true goal of stickiness is to encourage readers to browse your other pages and stay for a while.

Think of all the consumer sites that offer reviews, games, surveys and quizzes, chat boards and other features that entice readers to spend time on the site, interact with other visitors, and share their opinions. Not only do these sites build a sense of community and collect valuable consumer data, but they also dramatically increase the site's stickiness.

Stickiness helps visitors that come to your site get to know you, your book and your products/services/events better. Stickiness is also a measurement used in determining the effectiveness of your site. Sites with low stickiness are often not considered to be as effective as highly sticky sites because non-sticky sites don't create the opportunity to fully engage the viewer, making sales less likely.

How sticky you can make your site also depends on your target reader. Companies and authors that create products for children often include games, puzzles and even online worlds where their target customer (the child) can play for free. The child is having a great time exploring the site, but all the while, he or she is being exposed to branding messages and learning to associate fun with the product and company.

Sticky sites aren't just for kids. Sites that target adult readers may include quizzes and surveys, ratings, mini-games, celebrity news, fashion or sports updates, and other "time traps" that entice adult visitors to linger and take a break.

Is the topic of your book about business or pleasure? Either type of site can be sticky, but the approach you take is likely to differ depending on your viewer's interest. For example, a non-fiction book about health and wellness could have a site that features a blog with posts from the author and from other experts on fitness and nutrition, frequently-updated recipes and health tips, an exercise-of-the-day area, an ask-the-expert comment board, and even an "are you at risk" quiz.

Fiction sites can include can't-get-it-anywhere-else extra content, short stories, and even interviews with the characters. Some authors provide details about their world building, or hold frequent contests and giveaways.

Take some time to see what other authors who reach your target audience are doing. If you find yourself lingering on the site, make note of what has captured your interest. If you take a glance and leave, go back and figure out why you weren't intrigued. Put those insights to use in your book site.

Follow the Bouncing Visitor

"Bounce rate" refers to how quickly a visitor leaves your home page without going deeper into the site. It's the opposite of stickiness. Some of the reasons for a high bounce rate include:

» Readers find everything they need on the home page and aren't enticed to go further

» Users can't figure out the site's navigation and leave in frustration

» Links to go deeper into the site don't work, sending users away frustrated

» The visitor was misdirected to the site or realized it wasn't the desired destination.

Assuming your visitor came to the site he or she intended to visit, there are some easy ways to decrease bounce. Anything you do to increase stickiness automatically reduces bounce, so focusing on making your site stickier will help to reduce the bounce rate for visitors who meant to come to your site.

If your bounce rate is high, make sure all your navigation bars are easy to read and are clearly labeled. Users may leave the site because they don't know how to find content they wanted. Make sure that links work and that your site does not require multiple click-throughs to take visitors to their desired content. A good rule is to make all content findable within no more than three click-throughs.

Make sure the visitor knows what the site has to offer. Create a compelling home page that makes the benefit or entertainment value of your book tangible, and make it clear what else you offer inside the site. Use photos and attractive, easy to find links to encourage readers to take quizzes, read excerpts, browse products or find out about the latest events. If you offer multiple books, or if you write for multiple audiences, create a home page that enables readers to quickly find the content they want and go there in one click. Don't make readers scroll through products they don't want to find what they do want. Make it easy for them to find what they're looking for, and they're likely to reward you by sticking around and buying your book.

✎ ASSIGNMENT 18: Keep Your Website Fresh

- Visit your website and take an outsider's viewpoint. Does it pass the freshness, stickiness and bounce rate tests?

- Look for ways to incorporate ideas from this chapter to keep your site fresh, engage readers and entice them to stick around, and encourage home page visitors to explore other pages.

"Been There, Done That" AUTHOR TIP ✔

"If you are going to do it, do it right. Four words: maintain an active presence. Think of it as a column in a newspaper or magazine, and make sure you provide new material at least monthly if not weekly. Almost anything is effective — blog entries, contests, articles, moderated fan forums you respond to — whatever gets your personality across. The other thing a website should do is make it easy for your readers to find your books. If you don't self-publish, coordination with your publisher(s) is essential to this effort and the one step most often overlooked."

— *Toni Weisskopf, Publisher, Baen Books*

Chapter 19

Maximizing Your Website: Downloads, Freebies, and Give-aways

Your website can be a great way for visitors to learn more about your book and about you as an author, as well as any book-related products or services that you offer. Think about your site as an opportunity for prospective readers to begin a relationship with you, the author, and to sample and experience the book before they buy.

Creating an experiential site is also a terrific way to address freshness, stickiness and bounce, since a site that engages readers is likely to score well on all three factors. The more you can create an experience instead of a billboard, the higher your chances that a viewer will take the time to explore, which increases the chance that viewer will become a reader.

The Magic of Samples

Retailers have known about the magic of free samples for a long time. Think of how many times you have been offered a taste of baked goods, beverages or even entrees as you walk through a mall food court. If you liked the sample, odds are good that you returned as a paying customer to get more. The same principle works for samples of personal care and household products, trial subscriptions to magazines or services; many of us have discovered a new product through a sample given away at check-out, sent in the mail or handed out in the mall.

Brick and mortar bookstores have always provided a "free sample" opportunity for book buyers to browse before they buy.

Patrons are encouraged to pick up books, read a few pages, and flip through magazines before being expected to purchase anything. Many bookstores even offer comfortable arm chairs to entice patrons to spend even more time browsing (a real-world example of "stickiness").

As an author with an online presence, you will want to think about how you can offer readers the chance to browse before they purchase. This is especially important for new authors without name recognition who don't have an established following. Readers need to reassure themselves that the book will either solve their problem (if it is non-fiction) or entertain them (if it is fiction). Providing some kind of free sample is a familiar way to gain the reader's trust and help assure them their money will be well spent.

There's a reason that online retailers like Amazon offer a peek inside the books they offer. Customers want the chance to check out the contents and style to see if a book meets their needs before parting with their money. If your book is listed with online retailers, make sure that you offer the online sneak peek option.

On Amazon, that peek is only a few pages plus the table of contents. But on your own site, there's no reason not to offer the whole first chapter (or more) as a free download. Hook the reader with the first chapter (and the table of contents for a non-fiction book), and you're likely to make the sale.

Consider having a variety of different downloads, and change them periodically. This helps to keep your site fresh, and encourages visitors to return often. Other great digital previews that are free to produce and valuable for visitors include audio readings, book videos, or author Q&As.

Everyone Loves Freebies

There's a reason that the word "free" is the most powerful word in marketing. Everyone loves to get something for nothing. "Something" can be information, an experience, or a tangible product or service, but it must be seen as being valuable by the reader. Free samples are certainly one great way to encourage visitors to become readers. But there are other possibilities that are also easy for you to produce and free for you to offer, while providing a fun experience or valuable take-away for the visitor.

People love to take surveys and quizzes. Sites like SurveyMonkey.com and PollDaddy.com make it easy to do online quizzing and polling. Visitors enjoy the experience of finding out how they rate (always make sure everyone hears something positive along with constructive insights). Readers also enjoy finding out how their survey or poll responses measure up to everyone else's answers.

Your survey or quiz should relate to the theme of the book, but until you have an established reader base, don't require that your visitor have read your book to participate. Quizzes and surveys provide a short, fun experience that also helps to keep your site fresh and sticky.

Research shows that the longer a prospect handles an item, the more likely he or she is to buy. The longer you can keep a web visitor involved with your book (through downloads, freebies and giveaways), the more likely they are to overcome their purchase resistance and become a reader instead of a window shopper.

You can also create book-related freebies that add value for the reader without requiring extra costs for you. Create worksheets or a simple workbook related to your non-fiction book, or supply extra related articles, content that didn't make it into the book, research findings, white papers or case studies. For fiction authors, consider short vignettes that didn't fit into the book but add character insight, short stories, interviews with characters, or world building information.

You may also want to offer a free mobile phone application (sites like Liberated Syndication at LibSyn.com make these easy to produce), related games, or an icon, screensaver or computer wallpaper based on your book cover. Before using your cover art, check your contract or ask your publisher to make sure you have permission from the artist.

Great freebies also make it more likely that your readers and web visitors will volunteer to help with your marketing effort by sharing and forwarding the freebies to their friends. When this happens, your content has "gone viral." That means people who might never have otherwise visited your site will have the chance to get to know you and your book. It also means these new prospects will have been introduced to your sample and freebies by a trusted friend, which is the strongest recommendation.

Offer Giveaways and Rewards

Contests, giveaways and rewards continue to be staples of product marketing for a simple reason: they work. People love the excitement of entering a contest or a drawing, winning a prize or being offered bonus items as a reward.

While your book can make a great contest prize or giveaway item, I don't recommend giving it away on your own site for the simple reason that you want visitors to buy your book. On the other hand, when you appear on a radio show or do a guest blogging post, offering your book as a prize can be a great way to focus listener or reader attention on your book and generate interest.

Most of the time, sites will offer "no-purchase-required" random drawings that are pulled from the emails contestants send to a special email address. At live events, the emcee pulls business cards out of a hat to choose a winner randomly. There are legal reasons for structuring a giveaway like this, since you don't want to run afoul of lottery or gambling laws. When in doubt, consult a legal professional.

You can create a prize pack for even more attractive giveaways if you want to build your opt-in list. Think of how to make the reading experience more pleasurable, and bundle items like a ceramic mug, tin of tea or container of coffee and some fun extras like a bookmark or piece of biscotti for an inexpensive but attractive prize drawing and make it visible on your signing or event table. T-shirts, mouse pads and other small items also work well.

If you are sharing a vendor table or co-presenting with another author, team up to create a prize with items from both of you, and share the list of email addresses that participants provide. Make sure you announce a winner (first name only for privacy reasons) and send out your gift promptly.

"Push pages" have become common for non-fiction book launches, and are becoming more frequently used for fiction books as well. A push page is a web page or email message that encourages readers to buy your book by offering a number of free download rewards with the purchase of the book.

Usually, these downloadable rewards are excerpts from books by other authors that would be of interest to the same audience, but they can also be for discount coupons and other downloadable goodies. Because everyone who purchases receives the same reward, there is no contest or lottery involved. Push pages probably won't sell thousands of extra books for you, but they may increase your sales by dozens or even hundreds, which can be very valuable early in a book's launch when word-of-mouth buzz is crucial.

Samples, giveaways and rewards can be great ways to keep your site fun and exciting, while encouraging new readers to try your book and engaging long-time readers with something new. Adapt these ideas to your own book, and make your site a lively destination that readers won't want to leave.

✎ Assignment 19:
Using Gimmicks to Promote Your Book and Website

• Decide what you can offer as a free sample of your book and make sure the link is prominently displayed on your site.

• Look for opportunities to create attractive contests, giveaways and rewards whenever possible. Collaborate with other authors to create exciting prize packages and push pages.

"Been There, Done That" AUTHOR TIP ✔

"Make it easy for fans to connect with you. No matter how great your site is, readers are busy people, and they may only visit you once. Make sure you've got a way for them to add you to their online life with Facebook "like" buttons, Twitter "follow" buttons, or a good old fashioned e-newsletter signup forms. Nothing beats having a list of people who know and love your work who have opted in to hear from you. Make it easy to do on your site."

— *Alex Lencicki, Marketing and Publicity Director at Orbit Books.*

Chapter 20

And Now What?

Learning to navigate the Internet is a lot like becoming the citizen of a different country. Some things will be familiar, some will be very strange, and you'll meet a lot of people that you would never have crossed paths with back home. Creating a website and (more importantly) a web presence is the key to being a successful author in today's world. This book attempts to help you to take the first few steps, but the journey will require the rest of your life as a professional writer.

Long ago, I heard the proverb that "one can never step into the same river twice," meaning that each time, new water will greet you and the experience always changes. The Internet is very much like that proverbial river. It changes second by second, certainly day by day, with new people coming online and established web surfers finding new reasons to explore. Successfully selling books on the Internet requires that you set your raft afloat and go with the current, rather than trying to dam the flow. It's an exciting thing to be part of a constantly changing, dynamic, global source of content, but it can also be challenging and a little overwhelming.

You will constantly find new ways to improve your website and Internet presence, because new technologies, applications, widgets and add-ons are being created every day, and because people will continue to find new uses and make new demands of what they find online. Your site doesn't have to be perfect, but it should reflect a passion for reaching out to readers by being relevant, current and interesting.

There is no single template for the ideal author website or a proven map for the perfect online platform. Find what works for you — and more importantly, for your readers, and make it as good as you can by continuing to add and tinker. Don't forget to invite people at every opportunity to visit your site, and reward them when they do. Never lose sight of the fact that despite all the technology, the Internet is and always will be about creating and sustaining relationships among human beings. Keep that essential truth in mind, and you will prosper.

Writing is a passion. Publishing, however, is a business. The bald truth is that to be able to afford to continue your passion, it helps to be commercially successful as a business. Marketing (including your website and everything that creates your web presence) brings passion and profit together by enabling the largest number of people to experience and benefit from the information you have written. Good luck, and may you soar as high as your dreams will take you.

Author Website Development Checklist ✔

» Recognize that you are responsible for promoting your book, and that your author website plays an important role in successful promotion.

» Be clear on your goals for the book and your definition for success. Create your website to help you achieve your goals and attain success as you define it.

» Find out whether (and how) your publisher can help you, and then plan to do everything else yourself.

» Take an inventory of your personal marketing skills to know where you'll need help.

» Create your web marketing plan, complete with your Transformative Value, SWOT analysis and budget (time and money). Make sure you're clear on your target audience.

» Develop your ideas for content, bonus items, downloadable excerpts, event updates and other web copy to keep your site interesting and informative. Be sure to include your bio. Visit other authors' sites to get ideas you can adapt.

» Chose a domain name and purchase it.

» Determine the hosting package you need.

» Weigh your options: do-it-yourself template vs. custom designed site. Decide whether you want a blog as your main site.

» Add to your list of "must have" content items: links to your social media sites and your media interviews, an opt-in list builder (free download offer), photos, video, forum, shopping cart, Amazon link, bonus content, etc.

» Create a basic "map" of what should be on each web page and how you want visitors to travel through the site. Keep it simple!

Consider having special pages for the media and for people seeking speakers.

» Start writing your content, making sure that you stay focused on reader benefit. Don't sell—provide a solution or promise to entertain. If you're planning to write more than one book, start building expectations. Always provide value.

» Check out online shopping cart programs to determine what you need and what fits your budget.

» Consider what kind of downloadable digital products might fit into your marketing plan.

» Explore becoming an affiliate of an online book seller and consider creating an affiliate program of your own.

» Build out your News and Speaking pages with the information reporters and event planners need. Be sure to include a downloadable media kit as well as a speaker page.

» Create your own web video to welcome visitors and enhance the reader relationship.

» Record an audio greeting, a short reading from your book, or other tips.

» Make it a habit to take photos from all your events and post them online.

» Whether you build your own site or use a designer, be sure to plan good Search Engine Optimization (SEO) into the design.

» Use Really Simple Syndication (RSS) so your blog posts and Twitter tweets can keep your website fresh.

» Promote your site everywhere — in your book, in your materials, in press releases and email signatures, on signage and flyers, on your publisher's site, etc.

» Promote your status as an expert (after all, you're an author) by seeking opportunities as a radio, podcast or blogging guest, as a speaker, and as an expert contributor to magazines and newsletters.

» Use social media and social bookmarking to draw attention to your book and website.

» Make sure to tie your website into all of your non-Internet marketing. Use your offline marketing to help promote your site, and use your online marketing to leverage your other promotions, special offers, etc.

» Look for ways to collaborate and cross-market with other authors. Make sure you build it into your online marketing and feature the collaboration on your site!

» Keep your website fresh by updating content frequently and encouraging reader interaction.

» Make your site sticky with interactive quizzes, surveys, games, trivia and other features to keep readers on the site longer.

» Decrease "bounce" by making your site easy to navigate, keeping links active, and giving readers quick access to what they want to find.

» Reward readers with free chapters, downloadable extras, online freebies and special event give-aways.

» Realize that your site will always be a work in progress. Keep it fresh and interesting, and visitors are likely to become loyal readers.

About the Author

Gail Z. Martin is a bestselling author, international speaker and business consultant. She owns DreamSpinner Communications, and helps small businesses, authors and professionals get better marketing results in 30 days.

Gail is the host of the Shared Dreams Marketing Podcast and the Ghost in the Machine Author Podcast. You can find her online at www.GailMartinMarketing.com and on Twitter.com/GailMartinPR. She blogs at www.BigDreamsAndHardWork.com.

Gail is also the author of *The Thrifty Author's Guide to Launching Your Book Without Losing Your Mind* and *30 Days to Social Media Success: The 30 Day Results Guide to Making the Most of Twitter, Blogging, LinkedIn and Facebook.*, plus *30 Days to Online PR & Marketing Success: The 30 Day Results Guide to Making the Most of Twitter, Facebook, LinkedIn and Blogging to Grab Headlines and Get Clients."*

Gail offers online coaching programs based on all of her books. (www.GailMartinMarketing.com). Join her on Facebook at The Thrifty Author or The 30 Day Results Guide. Gail also offers two Meetup groups to connect with readers both locally and virtually. Find her on Meetup.com at The Thrifty Author Publishing Network and The 30 Day Marketing Success Network.

Gail is a frequent speaker for organizations that have included Microsoft Partner Edge Network, MarketingProfs, PR Newswire, eWomenNetwork, WriteWellU.com, 911Marketing-Help.com, SmartWomensCafe.com and the University of North

Carolina — Charlotte. She presents both live and webinar programs on social media, PR and marketing for audiences across North America. Invite Gail to speak at your regional or national conference.

In addition to her marketing career, Gail is the author of the bestselling *Chronicles of the Necromancer* fantasy adventure series (*The Summoner, The Blood King, Dark Haven,* and *Dark Lady's Chosen*) published by Solaris Books and *The Fallen Kings Cycle* (*The Sworn* and *The Dread*) published by Orbit Books.

Limit of Liability/ Disclaimer of Warranty:

While the author and editors have used their best efforts in preparing this book, they make no representations or warranties with respect to the accuracy or completeness of the contents of this book and specifically disclaim any implied warranties or merchantability or fitness for a particular purpose. No warranty may be created or extended by sales representatives or written sales materials. The advice and strategies contained herein may not be suitable for your situation. You should consult with a professional where appropriate. Neither the editor nor authors shall be liable for any loss of profit or any commercial damages, including but not limited to special, incidental, consequential or other damages. Nothing in this book should be construed as a guarantee of results or earnings. Your results depend on many factors, including your effort and skill. The Web sites cited in the book and all associated trademarks are the property of their rightful owners. Neither the author nor the publisher control the content on any third-party sites mentioned in the book and no warranty or guarantee of results is made regarding the products or services offered by third-party sites mentioned in the book.

All brand names and trademarks are the property of their rightful owners.

©2011 DreamSpinner Communications. All rights reserved. No part of this publication may be reproduced, stored in a retrieval system or transmitted in any form or by any means, electronic, mechanical, photocopying, recording, scanning or otherwise except as permitted under Section 107 or 108 of the 1976 United States Copyright Act without permission. No guarantee of results is made or implied.

CPSIA information can be obtained at www.ICGtesting.com
Printed in the USA
BVOW022253120212

282636BV00007B/24/P

9 781936 695409